Henry Bellyse Baildon

The Round Table Series

Henry Bellyse Baildon

The Round Table Series

ISBN/EAN: 9783337187309

Printed in Europe, USA, Canada, Australia, Japan

Cover: Foto ©ninafisch / pixelio.de

More available books at **www.hansebooks.com**

THE ROUND TABLE SERIES.

NOTICES OF THE PRESS.

I. RALPH WALDO EMERSON, MAN AND TEACHER.

"The little work displays an almost phenomenal insight into the genius of Emerson."—*Inverness Courier.*
"We heartily recommend it."—*Westminster Review.*

II. GEORGE ELIOT, MORALIST AND THINKER.

"The paper is a masterly one."—*Edinburgh Evening News.*
"We welcome work that is honest and fresh and suggestive and individual, and shall look forward to others of the series."—*British Quarterly Review.*

III. JOHN RUSKIN, ECONOMIST.

"Ought to be read by every man and woman of culture."—*Journal of Science.*

IV. WALT WHITMAN, POET AND DEMOCRAT.

The author's "style is clear and crisp, and he writes with abundant enthusiasm, yet with knowledge and discrimination."—*Pall Mall Gazette.*

V. CHARLES DARWIN, NATURALIST.

"An able exposition of the doctrine of organic evolution."—*Western Morning News.*

VI. DANIEL GABRIEL ROSSETTI, POET AND PAINTER.

"Mr Nicholson's Essay is perhaps the best of the series—eloquent and discriminating—and affords an excellent introduction to the study of Rossetti's works and writings."—*Dumfries Courier.*

ROUND TABLE SERIES.

EDITED BY

H. BELLYSE BAILDON, B.A., F.R.S.E.,
AUTHOR OF "THE SPIRIT OF NATURE," "MORNING CLOUDS," "ROSAMUND," ETC. ETC.

EDINBURGH:
WILLIAM BROWN, 26 PRINCES STREET.
LONDON: SIMPKIN, MARSHALL & CO.
MDCCCLXXXVII.

To seek the Grail *rode forth the knights of old
Of Arthur's Table Round, nor did they fail,
Wholly or all, who went, those champions bold,*
   To seek the Grail.

The G{\sc rail} *we seek is Truth—nor bought nor sold
In any mart; nay, Strength may not avail,
But Purity and Faith: and, as they told*

*Who wrought the olden legend, so we hold—
None wholly here succeed—none wholly fail.
So through the world's wide kingdoms we are bold*
   To seek the Grail.

PREFACE.

IN the Advertisement with which the first number of this series was prefaced, its aim was said to be "to give expression to the views of a number of writers, who, while representing divers and even antagonistic schools of thought, desire to give temperate and reasoned statements of their beliefs." The method adopted, so far as the present volume is concerned, has been to select for each writer such a great author as he was capable of expounding with most knowledge and sympathy. The object of this was to secure a critical estimate positive and cordial rather than negative or even coldly impartial. We wished the glow of enthusiasm and affection to light up our gallery of portraits. But at the same time we had no wish to descend to the level of mere sympathetic rhapsody. How we have avoided either extreme, if we have succeeded in so doing, it is for the reader to pronounce. That we have found favour with some, besides the usual evidence, we have that of very kind and flattering letters addressed to the editor or the authors— some from far over sea. Such things encourage us to bind together our *fasciculus* that so our kind readers may the more conveniently possess and readily transport it.

It may perhaps be well to emphasise the fact here, that there is no attempt at coherence of view among these essays, nor does one author, no, not even the editor, hold himself responsible for any heresies save his own.

An apology the editor owes to the readers of the series, and indeed perhaps most of all to himself, for the irregular and much-delayed appearances of the later numbers of this volume. He takes this opportunity of assuring his readers and himself of his entire innocence in the matter, except in so far as he may be blamed for putting his trust in reiterated promises. The real offenders, as so often happens, cannot be brought to justice. At least the mild-souled editor cannot find it in his heart to expose them to the fury of the erewhile gentle reader.

As a diffident dramatic author or modest stage-manager (if such there be) may feel a hesitation in stepping forth before the curtain at the conclusion of a piece, in case, after all, the audience are not so anxious to see him, as some of the sounds piercing behind the drop-scene would seem to indicate, so feels the editor in removing his not-very-carefully-preserved *incognito*. While doing so he may as well say that in addition to the first essay, he is also personally responsible for the sonnets on Emerson, George Eliot, Ruskin, and

Darwin. The sonnet on Whitman will be readily identified, from the initials and from its glowing and masculine imagery, as the work of none other than the "Surfaceman." The other poem prefaced to that essay is by Mr Robertson himself.

With regard to the appearance of future numbers of the series, the editor, under the sobering influence of experience, does not feel justified in making any definite statements. Something must depend on the public, something on the zeal, fidelity and success of contributors. If these conspire to set the vehicle in brisk motion, very willingly will the "ribbons" be handled, the box-seat resumed, by

THE EDITOR.

CONTENTS.

I. RALPH WALDO EMERSON,
  MAN AND TEACHER . .   *The Editor.*

II. GEORGE ELIOT,
  MORALIST AND THINKER.

III. JOHN RUSKIN,
  ECONOMIST   *Patrick Geddes.*

IV. WALT WHITMAN,
  POET AND DEMOCRAT . . . *John Robertson.*

V. CHARLES DARWIN,
  NATURALIST .   *J. T. Cunningham.*

VI. DANTE GABRIEL ROSSETTI,
  POET AND PAINTER .   *P. W. Nicholson.*

I.

RALPH WALDO EMERSON

MAN AND TEACHER

THOUGHT'S storm, alas, compass and compass-light
   Swept from the deck of my much-labouring bark,
     That still plunged shuddering through the surging dark,
Alone amid the tempest's turbulent might—
   And waste of restless waters, where no mark,
Or bound, or limit, to the straining sight
Gave pause or resting-place : the cloud-roofed night
   Hid all things but gaunt mast and cordage stark !

Slowly awoke around me points of light,
   Whither with joy I turned to find, alack,
     They rocked and veered : as beads upon a cup,
     They were of darkness swiftly swallowed up ;
   Until thy light arose to guide my track,
Unwavering pole-star of my spirit's night.

RALPH WALDO EMERSON.

THE human trinity, like the Divine, has its vicissitudes of prominence, and, as the Puritan worshipped the God of Judgment and Righteousness, the Evangelical the Man-God of Intercession and Forgiveness, and the Mystic the informing and comforting Spirit, so we have ages and classes of men to whom the physical, the intellectual, and emotional sides of our nature have seemed in turn most worthy of attention and culture. And, as in matters theological, it is a rare thing to find a true Athanasian to whom no person of the deity "is afore or after other," so it is seldom we find a man whose culture and development are thoroughly well-balanced and rounded. We see the athlete, who amazes us with feats of strength and grace of movement, wofully deficient in brain-power and in force of character; so may we find the man of intellect defective in physical and moral force and activity, and most worthy and even noble persons whose intellectual and bodily powers hardly escape contempt. Or, again, we may find vigour, health, and clear-headedness combined with a nature but ill developed on the moral and emotional sides. Natures thus thrown out of symmetry seem to be parts rather than wholes, and afflict us with a sense of defect and deformity; even as gorgeous hot house plants miss the grace and charm that greet us in many a wayside weed. When, therefore, we do meet a character in which at least there is a brave striving after due balance of development, we seem at last to have come face to face with true humanity. Such an one, to a large extent, we take Emerson to have been.

We must go back to Spinoza, "first cousin" (as Heine calls him) "of Jesus Christ," before we can find a character to compare for its startling purity and self-fidelity to that of Emerson. With such grace, as of Greek athlete, does the soul of this man move before us, that we seem to rub our eyes as though so perfect a presentment could not but be a dream, and a dream of divine imagination. We long, like the unbelieving Thomas, for tangible proof of his existence, and in spiritual and moral affairs the most tangible thing is a fault. How real and dear a juvenile *faux pas* would have made him! Why, the infatuated man actually paid his way and died solvent like any dullard! Oh for an account of some childish tantrum, some boyish escapade, some adolescent indiscretion! But no: no such concession do his biographers seem able to make to the human passion for frailty; he seems to swing clear of the ordinary dilemmas and impediments of life like a planet in free space. Born, he seems, finally to gainsay, with, alas, so few co-witnesses, the doctrine of human depravity, to raise once more aloft over the struggling hosts of humanity the banner of the ideal life, often trampled so rudely under the feet of divine genius itself. In many respects, doubtless, he was fortunate; born under a star of spiritual and even temporal prosperity. Yet the very purity of his nurture and surroundings made his moral successes the more difficult and the more truly signal. His was, to the onlooker at least, no crude choice of Hercules between voluptuous vice and pronounced, self-proclaiming virtue; it was rather the far subtler decision between a noble and a yet nobler course, a high and a still higher virtue. Yet it is possible that to his keen spiritual perceptions the contrast was broad and clear, and that he plainly enough saw the devil, though in the likeness of an angel of light. That the secret of his success was his utter and sensitive integrity, the absolute readiness and precision with which he obeyed the spiritual helm, admits not of cavil. Throughout he kept himself not merely *sceleris purus*, but *integer vitæ*. He trusted implicitly the dictates of his soul, and, as he says himself, "the soul may be trusted to the end." And so well from his youth up had he obeyed this divine helm that he seems to have required no acute spiritual crisis—to have "come round to the wind" in a fine curve rather than by sharp tacking; his soul's career being rather on the type of Buddha's and Christ's than of Paul's and Augustine's. He, as they, needing not so much conversion as enlightening and development, there being in such cases no μετάνοια, no repentance of former ways, but rather a "putting off of childish things." What was doubtless the crisis of Emerson's life, the assertion of his spiritual manhood, is marked by his resignation of the charge of Second Church, Boston. With a delicacy of moral perception, alas, lamentably rare, he had become aware that, in spite of the large surface of contact still existing between his spirit and the religious body he belonged to and instructed, it was no longer for his soul's health to maintain that position, and with a fine faith, which we trust may ere long be less exceptional, he believed no good could come to others from a falsity, however slight and pardonable it might seem. Without any posing as hero or martyr, he quietly resigned his charge, with a child-like faith in the security of his own future—a faith beautifully justified. Yet it would probably be highly unjust to suppose that this separation, so calmly accomplished, cost him no pang, or was decided upon without sharp inward struggle. For it seems impossible that a young man could quit a calling for which he had been trained, and for which, to say the least, he was far more eminently fitted than the majority of those who enter on it; could incur the suspicion or occasion the reproach of his flock, and could face a new and uncertain career without sufferings keen, though unbetrayed. It is, indeed, more difficult and painful to break through ties of affection and sympathy, and to give occasion for doubts and fears in those we love, than it is to stand singly forth against an unappreciative and hostile world, even at the risk of scorn, persecution and death. Well did the Carpenter of Nazareth know this when he said, " He that leaveth not father and mother is not worthy of me " We cannot doubt then, that, devoid of dramatic effect and effort as Emerson's secession from the church of his fathers was, it was an action demanding thorough manliness of heart, nor even lacking in the elements of heroism. Not but that he had his consolation, if indeed he was made at the time aware of it, in the faith in his character with which he had already inspired those who could most closely note his conduct; for it was some time after this juncture that Father Taylor said :—*

---

* Quoted in " Ralph Waldo Emerson : his Life, Writings, and Philosophy, by George Willis Cooke."

"Mr. Emerson might think this or that, but he is more like Jesus Christ than any one I have ever known. I have seen him when his religion was tested, and it bore the test."

From this point, so serene is his course onwards and upwards in the spheres of intellect and spirit, so blameless his conduct and so cheerful his self-devotion, that it seems as though he had then girded on some spiritual Excalibur, whose stroke no power unclean or evil could withstand. Setting no high worth upon immediate recognition, with no envy for the meaner heroes of the hour, full of an almost extravagant sympathy and appreciation for the best of his contemporaries, ever ready with generous praise and more costly aid for those that other men might have regarded as rivals, he yet surely forged his way ahead in public esteem, till he became the acknowledged chief of American philosophy and letters. He rendered his circumstances easy, not by amassing wealth, but by a wise and noble simplicity of living, a classic economy alike removed from luxury and meanness. Fortunate in his surroundings, as he certainly was, the serene dignity and singleness of his character seemed to merit and even demand those modest favours he sought at Fortune's hand. As with Ulysses of old, this Circe, who made slaves and brutes of other men, owned him her master. In matters mundane he had that balance and sanity so seldom present with men of genius, who are too apt to accuse fate for not throwing at their feet the gifts for which they will not even ask, still less do a hand's turn to obtain. It is, for instance, perfectly unjust to fate and the public for a highly original writer, determined to be true to his own convictions and genius, to inveigh against them on the ground that they do not pour riches into his lap. The process of recognition in such a case is *of necessity* a slow one, and this fact has been so often exemplified that all should be aware of it. He who flies in the face of universal experience has surely little cause to complain if he add another to countless instances! In playing the game of life we must fix our stakes, whether they are to be the counters of show and talent against those of popularity and success, or the solid metal of worth and genius against the fine gold of an immortal renown. We cannot pay in one currency and receive in another. Genius starves, harsh as it seems to say so, not because it is genius, but because it either will not sell itself (which is right), yet expects to be paid; or because although eager to sell (which is wrong), it finds no buyers. The fact is, genius is not a negotiable article, and the wisest possessors of it have lived, not by it, but by some minor skill, labour or accomplishment. Spinoza polished lenses, Socrates worked as a statuary, Shakespeare prospered as actor and stage manager. Following such wise examples, Emerson lived by farming and lecturing, not really upon his poetry and philosophy.

The following sketch of his home we cannot forbear here to quote from Cooke's life:—

"Emerson's house is of the old New England sort, large and hospitable in its very construction. A long hall divides it through the middle. By the side of the entry stands a table, over which is a picture of Diana. His book-shelves are plain, and reach to the ceiling. A fire-place fills one end of the study, and has high brass and irons; while on the antique mantle over it may now be found, among other articles, a small idol from the Nile. On the other end is a bronze lamp of antique pattern, such as is often pictured to represent the light of science. Back of this room is the large parlour in which visitors are received, and where many a conversational party has been held.

"The gate always remains open. The path from the house to the road is lined with tall chesnut trees. Back of the house is a garden of half-an-acre, where both Emerson and his wife are wont to labour. She is passionately fond of flowers, and grows them in profusion. Great numbers of roses are in bloom here in June, while there is a bed of hollyhocks of many varieties. A small brook runs across his land and pours into the river."

Here, in this homely nook, unfettered by indigence, unfevered by the thirst for material wealth, avaricious only of spiritual riches, yet sanely provident of the goods of this life; dwelling, as it were, on the hem of the garment of that wild nature he so loved and trusted; touching living and humble humanity in the simple town life of Concord; meeting in manly equality the purest and widest culture of Boston, and linked by intellectual affinities and lofty commune with the foremost and noblest men of genius of his time, he lived a life of physical, intellectual and spiritual health, activity and serenity.

The following sketch from the same source gives in brief the effect of his person and presence:—

"Emerson has a pronounced and emphatic face, not at all remarkable at first glance, but striking for its reserved power of expression. His head is high and well formed, his nose large, his chin strong, his eye gentle and searching. He is of a slender figure, more than medium height, head small, and shoulders remarkably sloping. His manner, though dignified, is very retiring, and singularly refined and gentlemanly. His face has a thoughtful and somewhat pre-occupied air, with keen eyes and aquiline nose. His countenance lights up with a rare appreciation of humour, of which he has the keenest sense; but his chief characteristics are beneficence and courtesy, which never fail, whether addressing the humblest pauper or the most distinguished scholar. In manner he is reticent, in general conversation he is not brilliant, and in ordinary intercourse with men he does not appear as a genius. Yet there is a reserved personality that is commanding, powerful, and charming. It is a personality that carries immense force, that moulds and sways others, less by dazzling brilliancy and tremendousness of intellect, than by the persuasive might of a pure, unadulterated, and perfectly loyal nature, which never swerves, which goes steadily on to the goal it seeks."

It is said of Moses of old that on returning from Sinai his face shone. Emerson seems to have worn a beam of that celestial brightness. Hawthorne and Frederika Bremer both speak of him as coming "with a sunbeam in his countenance." To Carlyle and his wife his sojourn at Craigenputtock was "like the visit of an angel." Such a man could be no mere moral paragon of correctness. He must have been the habitation of a spiritual force, the focus of the heavenly illumination of his day, the diamond from which blazed back the celestial sunlight, to which other surfaces replied with partial and feeble rays.

But of this light-reflecting, joy-dispensing power, what is the secret? Curtly and truthfully we say, "Health." He seems to have assumed from the beginning, contrary to orthodox teaching, that complete, three-facetted man, man physical, mental and moral, was to be treated as a healthy, normal organism, or one at least to which health and normality were possible, and not only so, but imperative. He asserted that physical disease is sin, and he characteristically, as we shall afterwards see, looks on sin as a morbid, abnormal condition of the creature. Nor was he in the least materialist in his views on this point, but rather spiritualist. He believed the pure and holy soul should so control the material form it has put forth from itself as its sensual dwelling-place, that it may always be strong and healthy: so he despised suffering and condemned sickness as a sign of the soul's discord with itself. He believed that human suffering arises from disobedience to laws that may and ought to be obeyed. When they are obeyed, the sickness will cease, and the weakness will be gone. Not but that he was too scientific a thinker, too keenly alive to the complexities and limitations of actual life, not to be ready to make at least the admission that this, though a general, is by no means an unexceptional rule. He would not, for instance, think of denying that practically from hereditary taint, from ill-training, from accident or from unfavourable environment, there are many persons to whom health is *not* a possibility. But he would doubtless maintain that even in these cases, the healthy spirit would tend to repair the defects and disabilities of the body or even mind. Also, while asserting the influence of the spirit on the body, he would none the less warmly maintain the converse. Hence his scrupulous attention to physical health, his practical return to the neglected Mosaic position that sanitation is a department not only of morals, but of religion.

Emerson evidently recognised that the end and cause of health is equable activity of function, and that so long as this is maintained, it is of little consequence how it is done. It matters little, for example, what variety of food is put into the stomach, so long as the stomach has the power of transmuting that food into flesh and blood and brain. So with the mind: the book we read is of less import than the intellectual power we bring to bear upon it. So with conduct: every phase of life has its possibilities which the vital soul can turn to its own nutrition. It is the inner force, not the external matter that chiefly imports us; to the ruined digestion, the lightest and most nutrient viands avail nothing; to the stricken intellect the simplest and the deepest wisdom is alike vain; over the blinded soul the celestial lightnings flash unregarded. In his hygiene of man, he would emphasize exercise rather than diet, as is really necessary, it would seem, from present human practice. The tendency of modern man is to eat too much, read too much, and act too much, —to digest too little, to think too little, and feel too little. Too much food, instead of strengthening the body, disorders the functions, too much reading, instead of quickening and equipping the intellect, tends to confuse its vision and clog its activity, and similarly, the man involved in a whirl of action of whatever kind, is apt to find his heart cold and his soul torpid. And, after all, the end of the business is not for a man to have done so much, read so much, and eaten so much, but much rather for him to stand forth after this action, this learning, and this consumption of victuals, an admirable person. This suggests the vital correction that requires to be made in the aim of our political housewifery or economics, viz., from seeking merely to provide a maximum of food and eaters, to aspiring rather to produce humanity in something like health and perfection. This is the duty which Goethe and Emerson recognised as being that of the individual in relation to himself; and while the former erred by paying a too exclusive and conscious attention to this phase of duty, becoming thus somewhat of a moral valetudinarian, the latter obeyed the same law in a more measured and natural, but no less determined manner. Goethe, in fact, pampered and coddled himself, if not physically, at least intellectually and morally, and by his anxiety after health, gave himself the airs of an invalid; but Emerson, possibly profiting by the other's error, treated his nature in more Spartan fashion, and thus acquired for it the hardihood that could laugh to scorn all petty and timid precaution. Goethe, for example, as an artist, failed in creative power, because he refused to abandon himself with sufficient completeness to the fierce Pythian inspiration which shakes and shatters the intellectual frame of genius; being too self-careful and self-regarding to face the suffering and danger involved. In like manner, in conduct he entertained the highest ideal notions regarding marriage, yet was so afraid of missing the mark, that he never succeeded in forming any but discreditable relations with women, his eventual marriage being as much a contravention of his own exalted rule as even his miscellaneous amours and intrigues. Emerson, on the other hand, gave himself so freely to his inspiration, offered so light a resistance to the passage of the oracular voice, that the tremour and convulsion of the devotee are hardly discernible; and to him purity was so spontaneous, so organic, that he formed lofty relations, and created an almost ideal household with the same ease as a crystal builds its polished facets or a flower unfolds its flawless petals.

But we might very reasonably expect to find, along with the Stoic and Puritan elevation of Emerson's character, a touch of that bitterness, that acidity of temper from which even a Milton is not free; that acerbity towards the great world of secular and profane persons too often characteristic of the saint and prophet, of which the almost cynic growling of Thomas Carlyle and the shrewish vituperation of John Ruskin are conspicuous modern examples. But of the existence of this in his case we get no hint. His temper, too, is the temper of health, virility, and strength. While against things evil his is the true poet's "hate of hate and scorn of scorn," he never descends from the lofty tribunal of judgment to cuff and revile the offender. He rather exemplifies the beautiful Christian maxim of "loving the sinner, but hating the sin."

While Emerson is essentially a philosopher in mental and spiritual calibre and character, he is a good deal else besides; and more than all, never expounds his thought in a methodic, consecutive manner. It is as though an animal or plant, instead of being presented for our dissection in its entirety, required also to have those parts re-collected and fitted together. His doctrines, taken separately, have not the distinction of novelty, nor is their interconsistence conspicuous. His thinking is in fact rather organic than logical, it is the *projection of his personality on the plane of intellect.* Hence he is never doctrinaire, never the puppet or victim of his own theories. Further, no man's spiritual or mental vision is so essentially *periscopic* as his. He is so keen to perceive the "other side" of questions and facts that it is not always possible to tell what the "resultant" of his thought is. He has called Plato's works "the Bible of the learned," and the same phrase very aptly describes his own; not only because of their intense illumination, but also because, as in the case of that volume, opposite theses might be supported from them, although certain main principles lie at their foundations.

If it were possible, and we trust it yet will be, to deprive the term of its present debased meaning and associations, and also to characterise so unique a mind by a single quality, Emerson might be called preeminently a *spiritualist*. To him spirit is the intenser, and even the prior reality to matter. To him the solid, opaque material universe is transparent; what he sees are the spiritual forces by whose action it is maintained. Yet his spiritualism or idealism is never strained, morbid, or fantastic, being always balanced by an equally keen realism: while his inner eye is awake to spiritual realities, his outer perceives none the less keenly and clearly the crisp, practical world of material facts. One of his favourite doctrines is that of identity, of the correspondence of nature and mind. Spirit or mind is the creative force, and nature the impressions, the "casts," thrown off by this ever active agency. Nature is the art-work of spirit, and is the embodiment of thought, as the picture is the embodiment of the painter's conception. The order is the same —first spirit, then matter; first imagination, then art.

There is, indeed, one doctrine for which he cannot conceal his contempt, and that is materialism, the theory of *material* evolution. This "quadruped opinion," he says, "cannot prevail." Cause and effect must always equate. Mind and matter refuse to be equated causally. No one has seen, or ever will see, the connection between phosphorus and thought, howsoever often it may be shewn that phosphorus is an essential concomitant of the brain. However we may struggle after finding unity, this eternal duality continually reiterates itself. This bipolarity is characteristic of the universe. These are the two rays into which the white light of Being was refracted by the creative prism. We must go behind that to find unity. For this unity there are many names, and perhaps of these GOD is not the worst!

But, while mind and matter have no visible causal

relation, they are correspondent.... As Emerson says, every thought has its rhyme in fact, every fact its rhyme in thought. The discovery of these rhymes is poetry, and it is the perpetual recognition of this that lights up the whole of Emerson's writings with a poetry of electric brilliance. This, and his other cardinal doctrine of "Immanence," which may be gathered from the following :—

"The essence of all creatures is eternally a divine life in Deity. Out of God nothing can exist, the outward world is a symbol of his innermost essence, and evil is but a privation of the fulness of his nature. The soul pre-existed in God, shared in his nature, was not then individual, but free and unconditioned, and as *immanent* in him shared in the process of creation. The soul is an efflux from God; but as no longer fully sharing in his nature it has become corrupt. In time it will return into the undeveloped Deity and be at one with him. Death to the individual self, surrender to God, is the condition of this return."—*Cooke's Life.*

It is well said that Emerson's philosophy is rather a theosophy. To him the universe is divine, and what we call nature, a partially and therefore imperfectly seen manifestation of deity. He comes very near being a pantheist, and indeed might be defined very nearly as a mystical pantheist, but he never makes that error of pantheism which confounds God and the universe. God, with him, is not the universe, but the soul of the universe, that which the universe is not, of which it is the manifestation and symbol. As he believes the soul of man to be the essential and vital element in man, so he believes this inner, spiritual world-life to be its essential principle.

"All goes to show," he says, "that the soul in man is not an organ, but animates and exercises all the organs; is not a function, like the power of memory, of calculation, of comparison, but uses them as hands and feet, is not a faculty but a light; is not the intellect or the will, but the master of the intellect or the will; is the background of our being in which they lie—an immensity not possessed and that cannot be 'possessed.' From within or from behind, a light shines through us upon things, and makes us aware that we are nothing, but the light is all. A man is the façade of a temple wherein all wisdom and all good abide. What we commonly call man, the eating, drinking, planting, counting man, does not as we know him represent himself but rather misrepresents himself. Him we do not respect, but the soul whose organ he is, would he let it appear through his action, would make our knees bend. When it breathes through his intellect it is genius, when it breathes through his will it is virtue, when it flows through his affection it is love."

Again :—

"The Supreme Critic on the errors of the past and the present, and the only prophet of that which must be, is that great nature in which we rest, as the earth lies in the soft arms of the atmosphere; that unity, that over-soul, within which every man's particular being is contained and made one with all other; that common heart of which all sincere conversation is the worship, to which all right action is submission; that over-powering reality which confutes our tricks and talents, and constrains every one to pass for what he is, and to speak from his character and not from his tongue, and which evermore tends to pass into our thought and hand and become wisdom and virtue and power and beauty. We live in succession, in division, in parts, in particles. Meantime within man is the soul of the whole; the wise silence; the universal beauty to which every part and particle is equally related; the eternal ONE. And this deep power, whose beatitude is all accessible to us, is not only self-sufficing and perfect in every hour, but the act of seeing and the thing seen, the seer and the spectacle, the subject and the object are one. We see the world piece by piece, as the sun, the moon, the animal, the tree; but the whole, of which these are the shining parts, is the soul. Only by the vision of that wisdom can the horoscope of the ages be read, and by falling back on our better thoughts, by yielding to the spirit of prophecy, which is innate in every man, we can know what it saith. Every man's words who speaks from that life must sound vain to those who do not dwell in the same thought on their own part. I dare not speak for it. My words do not carry its august sense; they fall short and cold. Only itself can inspire whom it will and behold, their speech shall be lyrical and sweet, and universal as the rising of the wind. Yet I desire, by profane words, if I may not use sacred, to indicate the heaven of this Deity, and to report what hints I have collected of the transcendent simplicity and energy of the Highest Law."

Such a passage clearly shows that, if this be Pantheism, it is not a Pantheism against which the charge of moral indifferentism can fairly be urged. The reason of this is that it recognises only as God, positive qualities, virtue, beauty, and wisdom, and acknowledges their opposites only as defect of these. In modern science, this principle is on all hands recognised, and no one would think of attributing to cold, darkness and silence, positive existence. They are simply the absence of those movements we call heat, light and sound. Why then may we not use the same method in theosophy? The analogy is as thorough as analogy can be, and any form of objection that applies to the one applies equally to the other. The only objection that can be urged is from the practical common sense point of view, and is simply that the fact of evil, cold, etc., being merely privative conditions, does not in the least effect their objective validity, nor lead to any alleviation of their effects This is, of course, no objection at all from a philosophic or scientific standpoint.

Upon these cosmic conceptions was founded or rather floated Emerson's beautiful religion, his lofty ethics and his profound, if general, political convictions, and not less his almost rapturous *rapprochement* to modern scientific ideas. His religion was a worship not of external nature, but of the Power it symbolizes and represents; his ethics an obedience to the same supreme voice speaking in his own soul, and breaking forth in flashes through the cloudy curtains of crass material facts. That the one was not unimpassioned and powerless, nor the other futile and misguided, his own life affords something like absolute proof.

On the nature of his religion there is no little misconception. Lowell, in one passage, terms him "Pagan," while there is no lack of earnestness to claim him as specifically Christian. Either term is too narrow to characterise so brave an attempt to create a universal and spiritual religion, a religion to which the labours of grammarian, commentator, and archæologist do not contribute the foundation, but which is built by the line and plummet of the human soul, a spiritual house from whose masonry no fact or truth, however stern or humble, is to be rejected. It is as though a cosmopolite architect had arisen with the genius to combine in one harmonious and consummate whole every precedent and local style. One recognising a Gothic window would pronounce him mediæval; another seeing a Corinthian column, Greek; and another a minaret, Oriental. So, with equal truth, Emerson might be described as Buddhist, Brahmin or Quaker. In reality, whilst trusting to that inner light in his own soul which he held divine, he fed it from all sources. He sought not for lanterns, as too many do, but for light. If he secured the pearl, he did not hoard oyster shells. His aim was to secure the essential and vital elements of religion, like the chemist who searches for active principles, and rejects inert matters. We may say that he emphatically believed in revelation, but not in partial and local, still less in mere historic and by-past revelations, but in a catholic, continuous, ever-present revelation. While repeatedly acknowledging the supreme place of Jesus among religious teachers, as he does that of Shakespeare among authors, Homer among epic poets, and Plato among philosophers, he allows only a difference in degree and not in kind, and rejects with absolute indignation the notion and practice of worshipping the person of Christ. In this no doubt he agrees with the Christianity of the Gospels, from which modern phases, if not, indeed, all post-pauline Christianity, differ very essentially. In these glowing and trenchant passages his position is clearly defined :—

"Jesus Christ belonged to the true race of prophets. He saw with open eye the mystery of the soul. Drawn by its severe harmony, ravished by its beauty, he lived in it, and had his being there. Alone in all history, he estimated the greatness of man. One man was true to what is in you and me. He saw that God incarnates himself in man, and evermore goes forth anew to take possession of his world. He said in this jubilee of divine emotion, 'I am divine. Through me God acts; through me speaks. Would you see God, see me; or see thyself when thou thinkest as I now think.' But what a distortion did his doctrine suffer in the same, in the next, and the following ages! There is no doctrine of the reason which will bear to be taught by the understanding. The understanding caught this high chant from the poet's lips, and said in the next age, 'This was Jehovah come down out of heaven. I will kill you if you say he was a man.' The idioms of his language and the figures of his rhetoric have usurped the place of his truth ; and churches are not built on his principles, but on his tropes. Christianity became a mythus, as the poetic teaching of Greece and Egypt before. He spoke of miracles, for he felt that man's life was a miracle, and all that he doth, and he knew that this daily miracle shines as the character ascends. But the word miracle, as pronounced by the Christian churches, gives a false impression ; it is a monster; it is not one with blowing clover and the falling rain."

. . . . . .

"In this point of view we become sensible of the first defect of historical Christianity. Historical Christianity has fallen into error that corrupts all attempts to communicate religion. As it appears to us, and as it has appeared for ages, it is not the doctrine of the soul, but an exaggeration of the personal, the positive, the ritual. It has dwelt, it dwells with noxious exaggeration about the *person* of Jesus. The soul knows no persons. It invites every man to the full circle of the universe, and will have no preferences but those of spontaneous love. But by this eastern monarchy of a Christianity, which indolence and fear have built, the friend of man is become the injurer of man. The manner in which his name is surrounded with expressions which were once sallies of admiration and love, but are now petrified with official titles, kills all generous sympathy and liking. All who hear me feel that the language that describes Christ to Europe and America is not the style of friendship and enthusiasm to a good and noble heart, but is appropriated and formal—paints a demi-god as the Orientals or the Greeks would describe Osiris or Apollo. Accept the injurious impositions of our early catechetical instruction, and even honesty and self-denial were but splendid sins, if they did not wear the Christian name. One would rather be

'A pagan suckled in a creed out-worn,'

than be defrauded of his manly right in coming into nature and finding not names and places, not land and professions, but even virtue and truth foreclosed and monopolised. You shall not be a man even. You shall not own the world, you shall not dare, and live after the infinite law that is in you, and in company with the infinite beauty which heaven and earth reflect to you in all lovely forms; but you must subordinate your nature to Christ's nature; you must accept our interpretations; and take his portrait as the vulgar draw it."

Here we have the true ultimatum of Protestantism, the trumpet-note of the soul's final declaration of independence; the announcement that it must and will live and grow by its own inner laws, organically, not to any form or pattern, however noble, externally imposed. The highest organisms are those that show the greatest amount of conquest over their environment, that live most nearly by their inner laws, and that which passively submits suffers immediate degradation. The lowest forms of life are the most elastic, the highest the most tenacious of their forms, the most emphatically *vertebrate*. So of the soul ; that soul is noblest which conforms to and depends on its surroundings the least, that has the strongest spiritual backbone. Of Emerson himself this is characteristic, and this he desires for all men. He demands of them that they shall assume in things intellectual and spiritual the upright attitude, that they shall not be babes and invalids and cripples, but shall stand straight and walk like healthful mature men. He announces that the hour of spiritual manhood has struck, and that, if the apparent paralytic will but rise and take up his bed, he shall walk. His is a boundless faith, not founded on external, historic, or pseudo-historic events, but on the nature of the soul. In biblical phrase he believes in that "light that lighteth every man that cometh into the world." Though unlike Elijah of old, he recognises God in the whirl-wind, the earthquake, and the fire ; like him, he recognises as his highest manifestation "the still small voice."* He accepts inspiration, not in the partial, tribal, and antique sense in which the orthodox hold it, but as complete, catholic and ever-present. Not waning as the ages go by, but rather growing fuller and clearer as spiritual evolution proceeds. His is the true doctrine of the Holy Ghost, in which the churches have so faint and fainting a faith. From the

---

* The following exquisite little story must here be quoted from Moncure D. Conway's "Emerson at Home and Abroad":—"Emerson loved to quote the words of Mary Rotch, whenever conversation threatened to become too theological. On one occasion, I remember an interval of silence, after which he said—'Mary Rotch told me that her little girl one day asked if she might do something.' She replied, 'What does the voice in thee say?' The child went off, and after a time returned to say, 'Mother, the little voice says, No.' 'That,' said Emerson, 'starts the tears to one's eyes.'"

smouldering fires of Quakerism he has snatched these embers and blown them into flame and brightness. From the New England martyrs, whom his Puritan forefathers condemned, has passed to him this priceless spiritual heirloom.

Not the least liable to be misunderstood, by devout persons, of all Emerson's positions, is that which he occupies respecting prayer. Beginning by objection to and discontinuance of formal prayer in public worship, or at stated times, he finally abandons the practice himself; this objection and abandonment arising, not in any degree from scepticism, still less from indifference or impiety, but from an exalted spiritual conception of the nature and office of that exercise. Prayer for temporal good and specific favours he regarded as mere mendicity, nothing better than the importunacy of the wayside beggar.

"Prayer," he says, "that craves a particular commodity, anything less than all good, is vicious. Prayer is the contemplation of the facts of life from the highest point of view. It is the soliloquy of a beholding and jubilant soul. It is the spirit of God pronouncing his works good. But prayer, as a means to effect a private end, is meanness and theft. It pre-supposes dualism, and not unity in natures and consciousness. As soon as the man is at one with God he will not beg. He will then see prayer in all action. The prayer of the farmer kneeling in his field to weed it, the prayer of the rower kneeling with the stroke of his oar, are prayers heard throughout nature."

There are then with him two phases of prayer, thought and action, contemplation and work; it thus means spiritual activity, and in this sense the noblest lives consist of prayer. Thus with him life was a devout meditation and pure action.

We feel, however, that there is something defective

in this analysis, for is not the essence of prayer <u>desire</u>, firstly, in low and crude forms for <u>physical good</u>, and afterwards for <u>moral and spiritual well-being</u>? Ultimately, doubtless, *in the limit*, as the mathematicians say, the desire becomes coincident with the divine will, and thus ends in self-fulfilment. But, practically what is meant by prayer is an effort *to <u>bring the soul's axis parallel to the axis of the spiritual universe</u>*, or to bring the heart into harmony with the will and thought of God. As both action and thought demand effort, so does prayer, and every true effort brings us nearer the goal, as every stroke of the oar brings the boatman on his way. If Emerson, riding the crest of a great spiritual wave, found this effort superfluous, was it not because to his spiritual evolution had gone the prayers of generation on generation? Here, as elsewhere, he errs in expressing moral and spiritual facts too much in terms of intellect, in projecting emotion and spirit too much on a mental plane. This is a besetting vice of his philosophy, and renders it chilling and repellant to those souls which cannot share that intellectual ecstasy which is for him constantly supplying the place of more cordial emotion. This it is that leads him to emphasize the <u>impersonality</u> of deity; for to the intellect God does not appear as a person, but rather as a power, a presence and a principle. Nevertheless, the heart continually demands personality, and in the absence of a personal God worships some deified man. The intellect demands laws, the heart yearns for the response of love. Ascetic religion forbids the love of human individuals; the sweetest form of Christianity demands it as preliminary to the love of God; while rational, catholic religion scarcely distinguishes the two emotions. Virtually, however, Emerson often evacuates his position in this respect, as when he says we must yield to our emotions towards God, though they should clothe Him with shape and colour. But still he habitually distrusted mere emotion, and thus saved his own practice, if not his system, from the eminent danger of extravagance to which, otherwise, it might have led.

In *his* soul, at least, Reason held perpetual assize, and to her bar every action and emotion was finally brought. To the highest affection he announces limits—

> "Love's hearts are faithful, but not fond,
> True to the just, but not beyond."

The fact that Emerson himself never displays a very intense passion may be attributed to this self-discipline, rather than to any original coolness of nature. In all its tender, and sweet, and brilliant beauty, his "Threnody" strikes one as ringing too much of the philosopher, and too little of the heart-stricken parent. But when we read Louisa Alcott's account of her going to inquire for little Waldo, we feel how true and warm a heart beat beneath the mail of his philosophy. She writes :—

"My first remembrance is of a morning when I was sent to inquire for little Waldo, then lying very ill. His father came to me, so worn with watching and changed by sorrow, that I was startled, and could only stammer out my message. 'Child, he is dead!' was his answer. Then the door closed, and I ran home to tell the sad tidings. I was only eight years old; and that was my first glimpse of a great grief, but I never have forgotten the anguish that made a familiar face so tragical, and gave those few words more pathos than the lamentations of the 'Threnody.'"

The root of [modern] scepticism—and we may

perhaps say of all scepticism which is spiritually injurious—lies in seeking for a physical or logical proof for spiritual facts. Every intelligent person recognises the folly of demanding physical proof for intellectual truth. It is equally fatuous to demand a physical demonstration of a mathematical truth, say that parallel lines never meet, as to say with the disciples of Christ, "Shew us the Father, and it sufficeth us!" Like space, Being has three dimensions or co-ordinates, so distinct, so rectangular towards each other, that to express the one by the other is impossible. Equally impossible is it to describe latitude in terms of longitude, and to describe thought or emotion in terms of matter or *vice versâ*. As, mathematically speaking, we can only determine a point's position by giving the x, y and z, so every existence is related to the three planes of Being, the physical, the intellectual, and the spiritual. Yet this fallacy is the basis of modern materialism.

Though probably all men feel it, and thousands have believed and expressed in various ways the truth, it seems to have been left to Emerson to express with scientific clearness the fact that "the spiritual is its own evidence." In physics, we take the evidence of our senses, in thought we accept what conforms to the laws of our minds, and in spiritual matters we must credit our spiritual faculties. Thus, in the matter of Immortality, it is not to apparitions and resurrections that we appeal for proof, but to the nature of the soul which continually asserts its immortality. As Goethe well says, and as every one must realise :—

"It is to a thinking being quite impossible to think himself non existent, ceasing to think and live; so far does every one carry in himself the proof of immortality, and quite spontaneously. But so soon as the man will be objective and go out of himself, so soon as he dogmatically will grasp a personal duration to bolster up in cockney fashion that inward assurance, he is lost in contradiction."

It is also characteristic of the first order of spiritual teachers, such as Jesus, to refuse to put their conceptions of a future life into definite form, while it is equally characteristic of the second order, such as Mohammed, Dante, Swedenborg and the author of the *Apocalypse*, to go into detail, with unfortunate results. Emerson attaches himself to the first rank by a steady refusal to utter a word beyond the message his soul has received. He is content with a broad faith in the matter, and says :—

"Whatever it be which the great Providence prepares for us, it must be something large and generous and in the great style of his works. The future must be up to the style of our faculties, of memory, of hope, of imagination, of reason."

He simply diagnoses humanity, and pronounces that there are portions perishable and decaying, but others of immortal stuff. Whether this immortal part will constitute individual persons, such as we conceive ourselves and others to be, he will not take upon himself to declare. In fact, he seems to lean to the notion that this sharp individuality is not permanent. May not spirit, as it were, *cohere in larger masses* in a different state? May not thus the sense of limitation, which now baffles and distresses us, be removed in a measure by larger accessions of power, as by the union of complementary minds? These are not his speculations, but he is careful not to exclude such. His doctrine of immortality is probably an exact analogue of the physical doctrine of the conservation of energy, except that he would not admit any such damaging flaw in the spiritual machinery as the physicists assert to exist in the physical universe under the title of the Dissipation of Heat.* To those who realise the presence of mental and spiritual energies belonging to a different order to the physical, a belief in the persistence of these, despite the purely physical accident of death, must be a truism, though they may not be able to predict the exact transformation these energies may then undergo, even as the physical philosopher believes, although he may often be unable to verify it, that there can never be a real *loss*, but only a *transformation* of physical energy.

There seems to have been somewhat of a change in Emerson's view of this great human problem, and certainly he latterly leaned very much more towards a belief in a personal, individual immortality than in his earlier years, and this is apparent before any wane or decay was traceable in his intellectual powers.

Emerson's method of teaching is assertive and oracular, rather than argumentative and logical. Like all great moral and religious teachers, he declines mere argument, despises proof, and rejoices in paradoxes, in symbols, analogies and similes. He maintains that the reason should recognise truth at sight, as the eye discerns light and colour. His sources for the discovery of truth were twofold, although the truths he sought were chiefly of the same nature—viz., intuitional,—the sayings of great and wise and holy men, and the whisperings of his own meditative soul, or rather of that Over-soul, that universal spirit, whose voice he held to be always

---

* We cannot help feeling a sort of intellectual grudge against this notion of the Dissipation of Heat, and the consequent running down of the physical mechanism. There is something so unsymmetric in it that we look forward (while respecting the brilliant guesses of Rankin and Siemens) to the advent of a more cyclic mind to trace the return of this now imperfect curve.

recognisable to the soul, whenever heard. Among writers of the intuitional order his reading was very extensive. Swedenborg, Boehmen, Eckhart, and many other mystics were his study and delight, the sacred books of the East, the mystic poetry of Persia, the myths of Egypt and Greece, Neo-platonist speculation, Norse legends, and saintly maxims and visions, were to him living and fertile, instinct with beauty and wisdom, informed with significance and instruction. And from these so diverse sources he not only collected a vast and unique treasury of ideas, images, and felicitous and weighty sayings, but he also thus fanned the flame of his own inspiration, keeping up in himself that vital activity of soul, which enabled it to flash out kindred truths. The result of this is that, while no one quotes more profusely (among moderns), no modern produces a greater impression of originality; because, beside the gold and gems " of purest ray," which he scatters so lavishly through his writings, he can place gold of equal purity, and gems of equal lustre, new from the crucible of his own spirit.

In Emerson the faith of the child and the philosopher are united, no soul is there so absolutely intrepid in its encounter with new facts, who prepares so hospitable entertainment for novel truths. He may be said to *keep open house for truth.* So strong his faith, so ideal his intellect, that no fact can be sufficiently crass to resist this powerful solvent. As a metal, rigid and resisting at all ordinary temperatures, is readily overcome, and reduced to a mobile and fluid form by intense heat, so the harsh fact becomes suddenly and strangely pliant and ductile in the furnace of Emerson's intense spirit and fervid thought.

This faith it is that enables him to offer so frank a welcome to those truths which for other minds have only terror and repulsion. He is thus the most scientific of philosophers, not only from his method, but still more from his prevailing mood.

<blockquote>
"Fear not," he says in his 'Essay on Circles,' "the new generalization. Does the fact look crass and material, threatening to degrade thy theory of spirit? Resist it not; it goes to refine and raise thy theory of matter just as much."
</blockquote>

Heine classifies the human race under the two terms, Nazarene and Hellene; meaning by Nazarene the rigid, correct, moral, ascetic, and harsh natures, strong in the severer virtues, but defective in tolerance and grace; and by Hellene, the easy, lax, sensuous, polished and genial, who, being weak in self-denying power, shine in pleasant and social virtues, and atone for their errors by charity and grace. The one class inspires respect and moral admiration, the latter win us in spite of ourselves, by the charm of their bearing, and the beauty of their manners. Historically, we can best match these terms by Puritan and Cavalier, John Knox and Mary Stuart; and while we revere and honour the one, we cannot repress our sympathy with, if not our love to, the other. Emerson, both in his character and his works, comes nearer perhaps than any other to a synthesis of these two elements. The one class pursue the good to the sacrifice of the fair, the other the beautiful to the loss of the pure. He worshipped at both shrines, and from his spiritual eyrie descried the blending of these rays. It is in his extreme love of beauty that he resembles the Greek, but he lags in nowise behind Hebrew or Christian in his perception of the beauty of holiness.

The basis of his ethical teaching thus acquires a breadth not otherwise to be obtained. He is thus drawn into a sympathy and tolerance towards his fellows, very rare among teachers of so lofty a strain. As Christ recognised waste spiritual elements in the publican and the harlot, Emerson perceives misguided virtue in the ruffian and the libertine. He sees that crime is often virtue *thrown off the rails*, and that evil is good in the making. This contributes to that optimism which is so characteristic of him. To him evil is mere defect, a lack of the Divine fulness we see in beauty and goodness. There is no doubt an actual historic truth in the saying that evil is good in the making. The strong and great nations springs from the loins of outlaws, thieves and barbarians. But, unfortunately, there is also the recoil from the good back to evil, so that sometimes good seems also to be evil in the making. To any one urging the problem of the existence of evil we should say, What right have you to expect to find in the world of fact that which is absolutely inconceivable to the mind? It is not possible to know good apart from evil, to see bravery apart from danger, endurance without pain, virtue without temptation. Truly it is a pusillanimous spirit that would itself evade this most thrilling of conflicts which life presents, and if we are prepared ourselves to brave it, should we not after all be content that our brethren should brave it also?

The real foundation of optimism is that innate faith of the soul that, after all, things must go well; its refusal ever to embrace the belief that the final goal and consummation of things can be otherwise than good. The soul persistently recoils from creeds that deny this. Materialism and Comtism, if they deny such hope to the individual, all the more loudly proclaim it for the race. Emerson's optimism is the free swing of this feeling, the reiteration of this assertion of the soul's faith, and against this he does not admit the validity of hostile facts. This faith, he says, is a spiritual fact. Spirit is the controller of matter, the real force of things. You credit outward experience and material phenomena; I the inward light and spiritual phenomena.

Few things are so difficult as to give a systematic exposition of Emersonian ethics. Never systematic in his own treatment of a subject, careless of consistency, that "hobgoblin of little minds," it would require a very long and exhaustive study to reduce this brilliant chaos to order. While avowedly accepting the doctrine of "renunciation," he accepts it rather in the sense of Geothe than in that of St. Paul. His renunciation appears to mean the abandonment of narrow and private ends for broad and public ones. You are to renounce yourself individually, but re-accept and assert yourself as a member of the race, an utterance, a manifestation of the "Over-soul." This distinction is subtle, but not, therefore, unreal. Could it be but grasped by many a loyal heart in this country, it would be saved from barren extravagances of conduct. The doctrine of mere self-denial, or mere self-mortification, is not only pernicious, but to good ends futile. It results in a moral asceticism, and starves the mind and spirit as well as the body.

Mere self-denial and mortification, instead of delivering us from that selfishness and self-concentration, which it is necessary to be delivered from in order to have that freedom which the Bible says belongs to the "sons of God," fastens it around us the more closely, and the more subtly. What we must, and indeed, in our higher and saner moments do strive to be rid of, is the importunacy and tyranny of self-seeking desires, desires which clamour for private advantage, pleasure or satisfaction. Such desires are somewhat like ill-trained children, who the more they are noticed either by way of praise and indulgence, or of blame and correction, the more obstreperous and unmanageable they become. They behave best with, and respect most, those adults who ignore them rather than chide them. So to study one's desires and predilections, even if it be for the purpose of denying them, has the effect of stimulating their activity to an abnormal extent. Never, for example, did prurience of mind, if not indeed actual immorality of conduct, reach a greater height than in the convent and the monastery which were designed for their total suppression. There are tactics and policies in the realm of morals and spirit, as well as in that of daily action; and in this case the true policy is to direct desires to universal and public ends so to speak, to ignore rather than mortify those which seek a narrow and a personal gain. There is, indeed, no natural desire but has a legitimate rôle to play in life and culture, if only it can be levelled at broad and universal ends, and not at those personal and private. Law, morality and true civilization are all based upon the distinction between the individual and the public benefit. There is no action which is not right when carried out for a public end—from locking a man up for a night, or fining him a few shillings, to imprisoning him permanently or depriving him of life. This refers, of course, to the narrow, human public of a nation, or a city, or a tribe. But there is a much wider public than that for the ideal moralist to consider. His universal is wider than that of Comtist or Utilitarian. His is the spiritual universal, the informing, all-pervading soul, speaking in awful whispers in his own conscience, and in every man's, and in that of all beings, high or low, in which the faculty for apprehending it exists. Hence it is that a man is right to stand by his own conscience against the world. The final end, then, of this renunciation of private ends for universal ones is the acknowledgment of the supreme authority of the moral faculties. The wrong is identical with the private, the universal with the right. This renunciation means, finally, the choice of good rather than evil; saying to the one an everlasting No, to the other an everlasting Yea.

But the man who has made this great asseveration does not thereby lose his individual character, and this individuality Emerson would not have him blaspheme or deny. After Self-renunciation comes Self-reliance. This renunciation, so far as it is complete, brings the man into harmony with the universe with God. He is no longer fighting for his own hand; he is a soldier in the divine armies. But the more completely this has taken place, the more reason has he to trust that inward monitor whose voice he has now finally determined to obey. The more therefore is he morally self-reliant, reliant on his own moral judgment.

"With Emerson," says Crozier, in his interesting, suggestive and lucid essay on Emerson in "The Religion of the Future," "this virtue of self-reliance includes all the virtues, and he never loses an opportunity of enforcing it. He regards it as the basis of all character, as the essence of all heroism. The great men we so much admire differ from ourselves chiefly in this, that while we rely on them, they rely on themselves. To the literary man self-reliance is indispensable. 'Meek young men,' says Emerson, 'grow up in libraries, believing it to be their duty to accept the views which Cicero, which Locke, which Bacon have given; forgetting that Cicero, Locke, and Bacon were but young men in libraries when they wrote these books.' So little self-reliance is there in the masses of men that they are spoken of as the herd, and their circle of thought and action can be predicted as easily as the return of morning and night. It is this imbecility of the masses 'that invites the impudence of power,' and perpetuates slavery and despotism. But self-reliance, by breaking up the routine of thought, lets new light into the darkened mind, and sets the world spinning on the paths of progress. If, therefore, hero-worship has been the practical creed of the past, self-reliance is to be that of the future. But so closely does every virtue lie to a corresponding vice, that it is apt to fall into it. Self-reliance as easily degenerates into conceit and bombast, as hero-worship into flunkeyism and meanness of spirit. Still, by releasing men from their stupid idolatries, and opening up to them the essential riches of their own natures, it communicates hope, stimulates aspiration, and gives new interest and value to life."

There is here, of course, a very marked and obvious distinction between the ethics of Carlyle and of Emerson. The one emphasizing hero-worship, the other self-reliance. To both their minds, doubtless, the world of human beings appears as divided into heroes and non-heroes. The one says in effect to the non-heroic world:—

"Wretched, supine, blind, and foolish inanities, you have no heroic stuff in your composition. One position only is becoming to you. To your knees, and worship now and evermore, the Odins and the Mahomets, even the Dr. Johnsons and Voltaires, whom I set up for your deities."

Emerson, on the contrary, virtually addresses them thus:—

"O unheroic, unsatisfactory persons, I implore you no longer to commit idolatry in this manner. No more kneeling and bowing to your fellow-men, mere imperfect, flawed, and irregular splinters of Deity as they are. Rather tread the paths they trod; adopt their methods; become yourselves heroes!"

Ethically, there may be value in both methods, nor are they so incompatible as might appear, but it goes without saying which is the more inspiring, which the more likely to result in producing heroes. Emerson has no better opinion of the mass of men, as they are, than has Carlyle, but he has more hope of them, sees greater capacity in them. He believes that the secret of their moral and spiritual poverty and meanness lies in a certain pusillanimity of soul, a lack of courage and belief in themselves, which is in great measure the result of that hero-worship Carlyle is so anxious to revive. Carlyle defines idolatry as the worship of a mere simulacrum, a mock-deity. Emerson goes further, and condemns the worship of the human, on the ground of its imperfection, its partiality. Perfect heroes, he says, do not exist.

"A man is like a bit of Labrador spar, which has no lustre as you turn it in your hand, until you come to a particular angle, then it shows deep and beautiful colours. There is no adaptation or universal applicability in man, but each has his special talent (intellectual or moral), and the mastery of successful men consists in keeping themselves when and where that turn shall oftenest be practised."

Rightly understood, and regarded in due relation to the other elements in Emerson's system of ethics, there is little danger and much edification in this doctrine of self-reliance. For we must remember that it is to be taken in conjunction with that of renunciation, it is the self-reliance, not of the worldling but of the saint, or in evangelical terminology the "converted;" it is not so much a reliance upon one's self individually as upon the divine voice in ourselves; not on ourselves as private human units, but on ourselves as parts in the mighty system of things. In theological language it is reliance, not upon ourselves, but upon "the grace of God that is given us."

Following upon the doctrine of self-reliance comes that of self-development, the statement that our duty lies, not in conforming ourselves to others as models, but in the development of those powers, of that individuality, which is given to each, and to none else.

As every organism has an inner law of its own nature which it fulfils, in as far as its environment permits, so every human being should strive to conform to his or her ideal, in as far as circumstances render it possible. The art of life, no more than the aim of true art, is to be mere imitation. Life is the factory of character, and we are to make it not a mere factory in the modern sense, but rather a studio, whence issue true creations of original and distinct design. We do not wish to turn out St. Pauls or St. Augustines, Luthers and Calvins, Bonapartes and Fredericks, Shakespeares and Goethes, by the dozen or score, but spiritual and intellectual beings as noble or unique as they.

Goethe it was who became the great apostle and exemplar of the important and neglected ethics of the "Duty to one's self." An already distinguished friend once said to me that he was more impressed by Lewes's "Life of Goethe" than by the Gospel story. The remark is likely to be sincere and also true; for in reality the gospel-ethic has so permeated Christendom, that by a sort of spiritual "adaptation," human natures are now either in harmony with it, or become fenced and hardened against it. It can never be read as a really fresh narrative, so much is it in the very blood of the race, so often have we perused it in the persons of our ancestors. But in Goethe was found a comparatively fresh moral impulse, a new ethical point of view. Hitherto our relations to God and our neighbour had given us our stand-points; now we are asked to look nearer home. We can well understand, then, how a mind, in search for new light upon the most complex of problems, the conduct of life, should be struck, and even inspired, by the new outlook, the fresh impulse. Personally, Goethe doubtless pampered his individuality, and never fairly realised the truth that self-sacrifice may be the best self-culture. But Emerson, in this respect, excelled his master, and if any man ever did, fulfilled his duty to himself, thus best fulfilling his duty to his fellow-men and his Maker; for we are a trust to ourselves, and our best service to our neighbour is to give him a good and wise neighbour in our own person. For not our talent merely, not our attention, or even our affection, not our wealth or our labour, are the best gifts we can bestow upon our fellows. *Character*, after all, is the great gift. The great man bequeathes us, not wealth which corrupts like hoarded Manna, but the high achievement, the noble life, the brave example. Quite just, after all, is it, that men should be ungrateful to those who give them money, promotion, and such gifts. Those who bestow them should expect no gratitude, should rather be grateful if they can find worthy recipients. But the whole world is grateful to its real benefactors, to the men of genius and character who have added to the conquests of humanity, have discovered Indias and Americas for the spirit of man to possess. As we must deny ourselves to possess ourselves, so often, in order to bestow ourselves, must we refuse ourselves. If we are at the beck and call of our neighbour for every trifle, we are useless to him in his extremity. In a thousand petty kindnesses we have allowed him to filch the moral fortune we could have bequeathed him and his heirs.

These doctrines of self-reliance and self-development are emphasized by Emerson, not because they are incapable of abuse, but because they best meet, to his thinking, the spiritual defects of the time. Emerson's ethic is too wide and spiritual to be formulated in a series of propositions. It is for the Reason, not the Understanding—it must be imbibed and digested for us to receive its true effect. It affects us by a sort of spiritual contagion, more than by formal commandment. We must read and re-read, and steep ourselves in his writings before we acquire their true flavour, and the capacity for understanding them. Not that Emerson is abstract and merely metaphysical. No one can speak in more homely and practical fashion, and amidst all his splendid generalisation, swoop down with more absolute precision on particulars. While you fancy he is soaring in the zenith of ideal morality, he suddenly transfixes with a sharp pang the most secret sin in your bosom. His moral perceptions have the keenness of steel, the speed of lightning. He maintains somewhere the vainness of hypocrisy; that the character reveals itself continually in spite of every effort, and we can well imagine how true that was for him, how transparent the man became before this penetrating glance. For him the human being is like a skeleton-clock—every spring, and pivot, and screw, and cog open to the light of day. Had he sounded the depths of passion, which he has not, his penetration into human nature would threaten the supremacy of Shakespeare himself.

The transition from Emerson's ethics to his politics is not difficult to make; seeing that really the same fundamental ideas underlie them. They are both *ideal*, and intentionally so. His object is to inspire with principles, not to inform with maxims. He does not wish to create a system of politics, but to call into being noble politicians. He acknowledges how little there is in political forms, he acknowledges the evils of democracy, the dangers of republics, and yet bates no jot of his faith in political progress and in the republican as the best form for modern government. Upon his philosophy and religion and ethic he founded his politics. Despite all discouragements, he never loses faith. Distrusting mere political arrangement and contrivances; ballot-boxes, universal suffrages, etc., as deeply as Carlyle himself, he perceives that they only require a noble nation to make them noble, a pure sentiment to make them pure, a wise constituency to make them oracles. Hence it is, that while our English prophets and teachers tend to become, and do almost to a man become, reactionary, and that violently and even blindly, Emerson never flinches from his onward course, and for ever befriends reform. The emancipation of the slaves, the enfranchisement of women, the education of the people, even Free Trade, all receive from him cordial welcome. Philosopher and servant of the muse, as he was sworn to be, he yet stepped froward at the most perilous moment to the aid of the Abolitionists.

The state, Emerson holds, does not make the people, but the people the state. Laws are the expression of the average moral sentiment. They can never be enforced against the moral sentiment of a people except for a very brief period. The condition of Ireland well exemplifies this.* The main difficulty in carrying out the law arises from the fact that the mass of the people do not reckon as crimes what the law reckons as crimes, and therefore it is that they are not behind the law, enforcing it by their consent, but either against it or indifferent. The excuse and the justification of the use of force and exceptional legislation arises from the fact that the natural sentiments of the people have not been allowed free play, that they are terrorised by force in a form more terrible than that supporting the law itself. The ideal political system is that in which the laws can most readily be adapted to the moral conditions of the people; or when, if possible, the legislative body is ahead of the people in morals and intelligence, so that this moral progress may be prepared for, or even by a little anticipated. The advantage of a popular form of government lies in the fact that the moral sentiment of the people, as of the individual, is always ahead of its practice; so that we legislate against vices which we have not yet abandoned, while this legislation again tends to educate the moral sentiment, to elevate it to a higher platform. It is like ascending an Alpine ice-wall. The place cut for the hands afterwards supports the feet, and so progress is made. The weakness of popular government, again arises from the folly of masses and majorities. But the majorities are in the wake of the wiser minority, and eventually, in healthy states, follow them.

Emerson's belief in the possibility of an ideal, or, at

* Fortunately not as well *now* as when this passage was penned; but we have a renewed illustration in the disaffection of the Highland Crofter.

least, an excellent state, is founded on his faith in the capacities of man. He sees, despite all disadvantages, a certain capacity for greatness, for heroism, in every man, and does not see why, under better conditions, this development of it might not become the rule rather than the exception. He believes that this heroism, which surprises us now and again on great occasions and emergencies should become common and continuous. If one man of a group of navvies (like Mr. Anderson's immortal Jack Chiddy "), can be found to risk and sacrifice his life for the safety of others, why despair of having a whole group equally heroic, or of having a life a continuous heroism?

While Emerson has no faith in political panaceas, in the new formulas of the Radical, any more than in the old formulas of the Conservative, he counsels that there should be no repression of noble attempts, no contempt or discouragement of generous schemes. He would oppose no reform, however fanatic and narrow its advocates, if it were a real reform. While he will not identify himself with any *ism*, he is content they should do their work and cease to be.

Of some authors we feel that their works are the best of them, that their lives and characters are but shabby and sorry comrades to their literary genius. Not so in the case of Emerson. We recur from the study of any aspect of his works with freshened pleasure to the contemplation of the man. In no relation do we find him failing; as son, as husband, as father, as friend, as citizen, his conduct responds to our expectations. Defects he may have had in each of these, but that he was a reverent and affectionate son, a loving and loyal husband, a wise and kindly father, a warm and faithful friend, and a worthy and dutiful citizen, there appears no cause to doubt. On the first three, his family relations, it is not necessary to say more than this, that it is by no means rare for a man showing a fair face, turning his best side to an admiring public, to darken with domestic vices, or at least to chill with neglect, the home circle he should warm and brighten. There are, however, many who shine in some, if not all these aspects, but it is but seldom, if ever, that we meet with our ideal of a friend. Beautifully as Emerson has written on the subject of friendship, he has thrown his writings into the shade by his noble practice. No man had truer, more generous and beautiful relations to his literary contemporaries. It was no Grub Street that he inhabited; and if he erred occasionally in over-estimating his friend, it was a generous and goodly error. Among Americans he held fine relations with the best of his day, with Longfellow, Holmes, Thoreau, Hawthorne, Channing, Margaret Fuller, and many more; among his English friends he numbered the chief in literature, philosophy and science. *He* was the prophet, *his* the shrine, to which the literary pilgrim was most drawn when, seeking light and strength, or full of eager gratitude, he crossed Atlantic billows. Tyndall declares that he owes all he has achieved to the inspiration of Emerson—and he wrote in his copy of "Nature," "*purchased by Inspiration.*" But the most notable of all Emerson's friendships is that with Thomas Carlyle. No contrast could be greater than that of the natural characters and dispositions of the men. It was only their strong, spiritual sympathies (amid strong and wide opinional differences), and their Olympian intellectual elevation above their compeers, combined with the almost passionate regard that Carlyle conceived for Emerson, and the splendid loyalty, geniality and manliness of Emerson's conduct, that could have bound them so firmly together. The correspondence between these two men is admitted to reflect the highest honour on both of them. The perfect intellectual integrity each preserves, as of courtly combatants moving a sword's length from each other, shows the immense self-reliance, the iron intellectual backbone each possessed. There is a dignity in their relations worthy of their spiritual kingship; their meetings seem like a Field of the Cloth of Gold, without its barbaric pomp.

As a citizen, while avoiding the strife of parties as a sphere to which he was not called, he struck in with decisive Achillean sword at great crises, with a dauntless courage and calmness which themselves secured him from real danger.

But what finally may we say is the dominant, the pervading note of Emerson's teaching?

It is the assertion of the supremacy of *spirit*. He flies boldly this old ensign from the mast-head of his philosophy. Spirit he retains as the best term for that power by which things consist; that without whose action the universe would fall to dead dust: that pervading electricity upon the path of whose currents matter ranges itself. It is never mere force, but at the lowest, force plus direction; its highest, intensest form is in emotion and thought; its lower what we call purely physical properties. As we may say, the whole of a man is alive, although the *degree* of life in all parts is not equal; low in the hair, the cuticle, the nails; high in the vital centres; so we say spirit pervades all things, but not equally. The usual antithesis between spirit and matter, as separable, opposable entities, is false. As we can only know physical forces from finding material substances affected by them, and now resolve these forces into "states of matter," modes of motion," and so forth, in the same way we resolve spirit into "states of matter," including conscious and emotional states. But as matter has no meaning for the physicist apart from the forces of which it is the subject, so it is also unmeaning and practically non-existent apart from the spirit by which it is moved. The separation of spirit and matter in their higher forms is just as conceivable or inconceivable as that of simple matter and force in the mechanical sphere. Mentally, we can conceive of spirit, as we can of heat, light, etc., as a generalisation or abstraction; but we cannot conceive of its existing apart from the substance animated by it, any more than we can that of heat and light apart from a material in a heat-giving or light-producing condition. There seems to be an evolution of spirit as of matter, and what we call spirit *par excellence* is to what we call physical, what living organised bodies are to chemical atoms.

To use a mathematical illustration. Suppose matter to be represented by x and spirit by y, then every form of being is of the nature of a function of x and y, $f(xy)$, and if the simplest form be of the form xy, the more complex may be x^2y^2, x^3y^3, etc. We may pretty safely say that these factors have always the *same powers*; that when x is in a low power, so is y, and *vice versâ*. If, for instance, we denominate the chemical elements as a class to be represented by x^1, we may represent the forces to which they are mutually subject by y^1, and if we represent organised tissue by x^2, we may represent the forces it is subject to by y^2, and so on, till we come up to some being represented by $x^n y^n$, a form infinitely more complex in both material and spiritual evolution. But the higher we get the more pronounced does *spirit* become, the more does it *sway* the combination, so that it would appear as though x were a fractional form (below unity), never eliminated, but always *decreasing*, while y is a whole number (greater than unity) always *increasing* with the power to which it is raised. This is really putting in algebraic form the assertion of Emerson and all spiritualists (in the proper sense) that spirit is the most important factor in the universe, the eventually triumphant one, and, even from the beginning, the major. And he only is a real materialist who asserts that matter from first to last is the more important and potent factor.

This mode of representing being must remind us of the truth which Emerson never forgot, and which was at the root of that sanity which was so strong a characteristic of him, viz., that potent as the spiritual factor may be, we can never safely neglect the material; that potent as the heart and mind are to spur body and brain, body and brain must have due attention, due nutrition, to keep them in health.

Perhaps the most characteristic quality of Emerson's thought is its habitual elevation of view. It is not, like Carlyle's, the view of a man plodding the streets and lanes of life, but rather that of some superior being contemplating mankind from an aerial height, yet with a piercing vision penetrating to the soul. Carlyle's is the bleeding heart staunching itself with its raiment of scorn, savage in its agony of sympathy; Emerson's the calm intelligence looking back to the beginning and forward to the shining goal.

THE EDITOR.

*L*IKE as an eagle from his eyrie on high,
    Seeing far below the crawling ways of men
    On the flat earth—tarn, lake and straggling fen,
Lengths of slow-widening rivers winding by
    Hamlet and tower and dusky town, till when
They meet the sea's white surge-hem; so thine eye
    Took the world's doings in its lofty ken,
Calm mirrored in its own serenity.

Nor thus alone like him, thy fearless gaze
    Quailed not in looking heavenward, the Divine
Was native to thy stainless soul, the ways
    Of heaven familiar to thy spirit's feet,
    All baseness strange to that high heart of thine,
    All evil bitter to thee and virtue sweet.

II.

GEORGE ELIOT

MORALIST AND THINKER

GRAY in the gray dawn of an æon new
    A sybil sat, and from her lips there fell
    Grave words and sad, as to her potent spell
Uprose bright visions of the past that grew,
It seemed, to life again, till forth there drew—
    Yea, walked among us, as by miracle,
    Scholar and knight, lady and monk, to tell
The joy they sought, the sorrow that they knew.

Or changed the vision; the perplexèd hum
    Of daily life grew vocal; all the loud
    Struggle and strife waxed clear; the moving crowd
Was stayed for parley:—'neath the mighty sum
    Of evil and sorrow her sad head was bowed,
Yet on her brow smiled out the Day to come.

GEORGE ELIOT.

THE critic who passes under judgment the creed and teaching of an imaginative writer as embodied in artistic creations is often at the disadvantage of needing first to prove the existence of his subject-matter. He lays himself open to be told not only, that his interpretation of this or that work of art is at fault, but that he has erred in supposing that there is any definite meaning to be discovered. In many cases there is much to support such a contention; though the reply may be confidently made that however the consciousness of a purpose be disavowed, and the spontaneity of art vindicated, the *motif* of the artist must, theoretically at least, admit of an intellectual expression. With George Eliot, however, no such initial difficulty arises. So far from needing to establish the presence of a dogmatic and subjective element in her works, her disciples are called upon to defend her on the charge of having obtruded the 'moral' to the detriment of the artistic effect. Her philosophy, if not formulated with the explicitness of a definite creed, reaches us at least through no subtle extraction from doubtful phrases. Throughout her novels, the personal comments fill up the pauses in the action of the story like the chorus in a Greek drama. Nor are there wanting from other sources even more direct avowals of religious and moral conviction. If it be asked, 'How, therefore, is there need for an interpreter, when all is so full and simple that he who runs may read?' the answer must be that the reflection of an author's meaning through the medium of concrete images and expressions attains completeness according to the degree of preparation in the minds of those to whom he appeals, and that few of us can boast of such intellectual consistency that we can readily assimilate a fresh influence, and form a new resultant of belief. There are many readers of George Eliot in whose hearts responsive chords have vibrated as to the sound of a new music, but who shrink from the readjustment of their thoughts and actions which would be involved in an effort to follow her teaching to its legitimate issues. Such hesitation, however, cannot form a permanent mental condition. Conflicting ideas will struggle towards an equilibrium, and the privilege of the critic lies in contributing to the work of co-ordination.

George Eliot is the chief exponent that has yet appeared in the world of art of the new synthesis based on the scientific investigations of the present century. More than one critic has already pointed out, though none perhaps has carefully traced, the close relation of her teaching to that of Comte, Darwin, Lewes, and Spencer. The question of originality is always a perplexing one, and we shall best escape it in the present instance by disavowing all claim for our author to the first possession of any of the leading doctrines found in her works. But whether they were in the main due to her close companionship with the scientific thinkers among whom her lot was cast, or to the subtler influences borne to her as to them by the spirit of the time, we maintain that when passed through the alembic of her mind, these doctrines attain a consistency and a unity hardly to be found in the works of any of the writers above named. In her hands the new synthesis has challenged, and has successfully stood, the only test of its truth which can anticipate the final verdict of the ages—it has formed the background for imaginative creations to which the universal judgment has accorded a high place in the Temple of Art.

What is George Eliot's philosophy of life? To her, as to most thinkers, life appears as an amalgam of will and destiny, but it is in the interpretation of these terms that the distinctive element of each philosophy lies. To the understanding of her analysis of them there is necessary a general acquaintance with the leading generalisations of biological science, which may briefly be stated as follows:—

I. There is a continuity of law through all the phenomena displayed by living beings. The most complex ethical and social actions may be traced in germ in the lowest animal or plant.

II. All phases of life are ultimately expressible in terms of the relation between the organism and its environment, the history of that relation revealing a gradual evolution of organic structure and function under the influence of the surroundings. This progressive adaptation is attained in part directly by the balancing of forces, in part indirectly by natural selection—the survival of the fittest. Modifications of structure thus established are maintained by hereditary transmission.

III. The inner world of consciousness is correlative

with outward manifestations of life, and has thus necessarily the same laws.

These doctrines, embodying the law of evolution as applied uniformly to all phases of life, alike in their objective and subjective aspects, are the fundamental assumptions in George Eliot's philosophy, and find ample illustration in her writings. Such material, which to the majority of thinkers seems inadequate for even the most general expression of human life, affords to her the key to all its deepest problems.

It has been said that the two factors which make up the life of man are Will and Destiny. But these terms are associated with modes of thought where the conceptions they symbolise are held to admit of no further analysis. A more advanced philosophy has ceased to regard them as ultimate elements behind which it is impossible to penetrate, and seeks an explanation of their relation in a more intimate study of their nature. If the old nomenclature is retained, it is in an approximate and popular sense, and mainly for the sake of preserving the historical continuity of speculation. For the confessions of ignorance, which such terms really represent, there are substituted definitions derived from the exact knowledge which rewards scientific research.

Will, character, personality, is no longer referred to a special divine afflatus or inherent tendency, but is shewn to be the resultant of organic functions, or, to use subjective language, the general tendency of our persistent desires. The value of such a conception lies in the light it throws on the possibilities of modifying inherited nature. Not that the principle of heredity was unknown to former systems. In its physical aspects, as in family resemblances of personal appearance, it was too obvious to escape attention, but the supposed independence of the body and the mind prevented the extension of its application to all the phenomena of life. The fuller recognition which the doctrine can now receive finds due expression in George Eliot's writings. Especially in the story of Fedalma, the gipsy maiden, who renounces love and happiness in response to the call waking into life the dormant sympathy with her outcast race, which neither lapse of years nor change of circumstance can quench, she has given us a memorable study of the persistence of hereditary bias through all counteracting influences.

> " Lay the young eagle in what nest you will,
> The cry and swoop of eagles overhead
> Vibrate prophetic in its kindred frame ;
> And make it spread its wings and poise itself
> For the eagle's flight."—*Spanish Gipsy*, p. 152.[1]

In close relation with this deeper insight into the character of the individual element in human life stands her treatment of the complementary factor, the influence of the environment. In the older religions, destiny had varied in aspect from an impersonal and inexorable fate, regardless of human affairs, to an anthropomorphic being not inaccessible to petition, though arbitrary in action. The increase in harmony between man and his surroundings, due to the modification of organic structure by external forces, tended to push to an extreme the reaction from absolute fatalism, and begat a belief in a God whose beneficence was theoretically held to be unbounded, and whose action might be indefinitely influenced by all who possessed the necessary faith. The tendency to paralyse action characteristic of the older belief gave way to the opposite danger of an

[1] The cabinet edition of George Eliot's works will be referred to throughout.

excessive trust in human powers, in which we see the genesis of the Christian conscience, gathering strength from its self-confidence, but losing it in a morbid sensitiveness to failure in achievement. The scientific conception aims at adjusting the balance of truth by fixing the limits of action and reaction between the inner and outer forces. To the genius of George Eliot we mainly owe the application of this law to the higher phases of human life, [where for each individual the forces of the environment largely consist of the moral and social influences of his fellow-men. She it is who more than any other teacher has traced for us the complex interaction of human factors, the subtle weaving of the threads of destiny by unconscious hands into the web of our daily history—who, in showing us the mighty unforeseen issues of our tiniest actions for good or evil to ourselves and others, has taught us as far as in us lies, so to order our lives that we may not be ashamed.

"Men's lives are as thoroughly blended as the air they breathe; evil spreads as necessarily as disease."—*Adam Bede*, ii. 205.

"In the multitude of middle-aged men, who go about their vocations in a daily course determined for them much in the same way as the tie of their cravats, there is always a good number who once meant to shape their own deeds and alter the world a little. . . . Nothing more subtle than the process of their gradual change! In the beginning they inhaled it unknowingly; you and I may have sent some of our breath towards infecting them when we uttered our conforming falsities, or drew our silly conclusions."—*Middlemarch*, ii. 218.

Based on her perception of the possibilities of influence between man and man in helping to determine each other's environment, and of the unfailing rigour, veiled by a superficial indefiniteness, of moral causes and effects, there arises the fuller and juster appreciation of the Past, in which she represents a growing tendency of modern thought. This we may view under several aspects. In the history of Tito Melema she has traced with a master-hand the tyranny of our past actions, even the most trivial, in shaping the after-life to an inexorable sequence, in moulding the character in consonance with their need of justification. It is a truth she never tires of enforcing.

"There is a terrible coercion in our deeds which may first turn the honest man into a deceiver, and then reconcile him to the change."—*Adam Bede*, ii. 37.

"Our deeds are like children that are born to us; they live and act apart from our own will. Nay, children may be strangled, but deeds never; they have an indestructible life both in and out of our consciousness."—*Ibid*. i. 248.

"Our lives make a moral tradition for our individual selves, as the life of mankind at large makes a moral tradition for the race; and to have once acted greatly seems a reason why we should always be noble."—*Ibid*. ii. 88.

". . . . that inexorable law of human souls, that we prepare ourselves for sudden deeds by the reiterated choice of good or evil that gradually determines character."—*Ibid*. i. 340.

The essential continuity of past and present thus traced in the individual life, we find recognised with equal insight in the history of our race. With George Eliot there is no isolation of human lots. No life but is bound by numberless ties to every other; none so paltry and remote that it has not its share in the common history, and its genuine interest to all sympathetic souls. This view of the solidarity of our race, uniting all aspects of life through space and time in the bonds of a common brotherhood, illustrates and commends to our understanding the Positivist conception of Humanity as a collective unity, a *grand être* in which are gathered up the noble deeds, past, present, and to come, to which our race owes its well-being and progress, and in which we find the truest object of our love and reverence.

"A man conscious of enthusiasm for worthy aims is sustained by the memory of great workers, who hover in his mind as patron saints, invisibly helping."—*Middlemarch*, ii. 277.

"Let us raise a monument to the soldiers whose brave hearts only kept the ranks unbroken, and met death—a monument to the faithful who were not famous, and who are precious as the continuity of the sunbeams is precious."—*Felix Holt*, i. 274.

The high generality of this conception is tempered in the pages of George Eliot by the intensity and wide range of her individual sympathies :—

"Surely the only true knowledge of our fellow-men is that which enables us to feel with him, which gives us a fine ear for the heart-pulses that are beating under the mere clothes of circumstance and opinion. Our subtlest analysis of schools and sects must miss the essential truth unless it be lit up by the love that sees in all forms of human thought and work the life-and-death-struggles of separate human beings.—*Scenes of Clerical Life*, ii. 166.

It is in this relation of the individual to humanity as a whole, this expression of personal life as the reaction of egoistic feeling on social surroundings, that she finds the explanation of morality. *Conscience* and *duty* are with her terms which represent a general statement of organic action adjusted to a given environment, or, to use language of more special reference to the phase of evolution now reached, a statement of human conduct in harmony with social conditions. The crude definition of duty in theological systems of ethics, as obedience to the will of a deity, finds its scientific counterpart here in the doctrine that the lines of our conduct are determined by the past within and without us; that the structure of our brains, directing the motion which issues in action, forms a record of the experiences, personal and ancestral, gained in the conflict with external forces. The element of constraint, which at present belongs to our use of the term *duty*, is regarded as incidental to the struggle between the egoistic and the altruistic functions in the adjustment of a stable equilibrium. In the degree that social conditions approach a level standard, and mould individual lives into conformity, will duty become organic, and its distinction from natural action disappear.

Morality is thus virtually resolved into sympathy. Our feeling of obligation to act in certain ways merely expresses our openness to influences from the needs and desires of our fellow-men. [The course of evolution substitutes a common interest for an individual interest as an ideal for human life.] The consequent re-adjustment of impulses to a new system of conduct, in which egoism and altruism shall find a *modus vivendi*, is now in progress, and causes a period of comparative anarchy, interposed between the original simplicity of a life determined by inorganic surroundings only, and the final simplicity of a life harmonised with the widest social ideal. Conscience is the anticipation, more or less adequate in each of us, of this limit of human development.

"You feel as I do," says Maggie Tulliver, "that the real tie lies in the feelings and expectations we have raised in other minds. Else all pledges might be broken when there was no outward penalty. There would be no such thing as faithfulness.—*Mill on the Floss*, ii. 287.

"If the past is not to bind us where can duty lie? We should have no law but the inclination of the moment.—*Ibid.* ii. 329.

And Romola, in passionate remonstrance with her self-seeking husband :—

"You talk of substantial good, Tito. Are faithfulness, and love, and sweet, grateful memories no good? Is it no good that we should keep our silent promises on which others build, because they believe in our love and truth?"—*Romola*, i. 436.

But not to the heartless and selfish only is this lesson needful, and the young wife, whose love and trust have perished in the cruel frost of her husband's faithlessness to all noble aims, is sternly arrested in her flight by the words of Savonarola :—

"You are turning your back on the lot that has been appointed for you—you are going to choose another. But can man or woman choose duties? No more than they can choose their birthplace, or their father and mother."—*Romola*, ii. p. 102.

"You are seeking some good other than the law you are bound to obey. But how will you find good? It is not a thing of choice; it is a river that flows from the foot of the invisible throne, and flows by the path of obedience."—*Ibid.* ii. 105.

Many other passages from George Eliot's works convey the same meaning. She speaks of

"That knowledge of the irreversible laws within and without, which, governing the habits, becomes morality."—*Mill on the Floss*, ii. 31-2.

And further :—

"Those old stories of visions and dreams guiding men have their truth; we are saved by making the future present to ourselves."—*Felix Holt*, ii. 40.

The most definite utterance of her belief in the future of morality is to be found in the record of a conversation with a friend, in which she expressed her belief that the time would come when the impulse to help our neighbour would be as instinctive as the impulse to clutch at the nearest object when we are falling.

At this point the question must arise—What place does happiness hold in George Eliot's philosophy? Does she echo the stern demand of the old morality—"What hast thou to do with happiness?" or does she offer a more adequate solution of this problem which the world will not cease to concern itself with? To understand this matter aright, it is needful to consider the physiological and psychological view of life which she shared with her accomplished and gifted husband, a view which, if not formulated by them with the completeness it can now receive, was yet essentially theirs, and forms the only consistent setting to the doctrines above traced.

If life be proximately defined as *the form of force displayed by organisms*, or more shortly as *organic action*, we must be careful to make a distinction which is often neglected. The actions of an organism may be either *in* harmony or *out of* harmony with the forces of the environment. The laws of existence may be followed or disregarded; we may eat food or poison. We are accustomed to apply the word *life* to all the actions of an organism, whether they tend to further action, or to decay and death; but if we restrict the use of the term to the former class, we have a more strictly scientific expression of life as *organic action in harmony with the environment*.

Such is the only definition possible to the external observer, but to the organism itself life has also an inner meaning. All actions consciously performed, have a subjective as well as an objective side; action and emotion are correlative aspects of the same fact. Is there any broad general distinction among emotions corresponding to that between life-bringing and death-bringing actions? There is. The former class are on the whole pleasurable, the latter painful. This substantial correspondence has in past systems generally remained an unexplained coincidence, the apparent inconsistencies having absorbed attention, and even given birth to religions founded on a negation of any possible harmony between happiness and well-being. It is one of the functions of the scientific synthesis to indicate the essential unity underlying this diversity of aspect, and to attempt an explanation of the acknowledged anomalies. "He that saveth his life shall lose it" has not lost its truth, but a wider interpretation is now possible. The partial want of harmony is referred to incompleteness in the integration of functions; the organism is only approaching unity. The introduction of the social factor into human life, forming the chief element in our environment, has so modified the ideal as to demand a total readjustment of cerebral structure in harmony with it, and until a new equilibrium is reached, some discord is inevitable. The struggle of the egoistic and altruistic desires in which the genesis of morality has been traced, postpones the complete identification of pleasure and well-being. "Only when duty and love have united in one stream, and made a common force," will happiness and life be reconciled.

In the pages of George Eliot we shall not fail to find due recognition of the confusion which this radical change of aim has brought into human progress:—

"Oh, it is difficult!" Maggie Tulliver cries, in sad conflict with the love that came to her in the form of temptation, "life is very difficult. It seems right to me sometimes that we should follow our strongest feeling; but then such feelings continually come across the ties that all our former life has made for us—the ties that have made others dependent on us—and would cut them in two. If life were quite easy and simple, as it might have been, in paradise . . . but I see, I feel it is not so now; there are things we must renounce in life. . . . I must not, cannot seek my own happiness by sacrificing others. Love is natural, but surely pity and faithfulness and memory are natural too. And they would live in me still, and punish me if I did not obey them. I should be haunted by the suffering I had caused."—*Mill on the Floss*, ii. 287.

But springing out of this deeper interpretation of the present anarchy in human life, we find the vision of a millennium when peace shall again reign on the earth, but a higher peace than that of paradise, when to act will be to live, and to live will mean to be happy. The vision casts its radiance before it; even now we have a foretaste of such a heaven in the growing harmony of conscience and will, of duty and desire. Not the smallest factor in the change of attitude which forbids our shrinking from happiness, as from temptation, has been the wider conception of human life as part of a great organic whole, determined by unchangeable relations to the surrounding universe. Of this conception, to the development of which many workers have contributed, perhaps the most adequate exposition may be found in the works of George Eliot.

The most immediately useful lesson to be learnt from it lies in the obvious corollary that happiness can be increased in two ways only, by a change either in the individual or in the environment. We may, with the Stoics, seek content by limiting our desires, or we may seek a more positive form of happiness by striving to enlarge our opportunities. The stress which the theory of evolution lays on the influence of the environment as a factor in determining human life tends to give an increasing prominence to the latter alternative.

Effort is supplanting resignation; *Kismet* is no longer the final expression of religious feeling.

But the lesson is of still greater value in its altruistic application; it gives a rule for the direction of sympathetic energy. New vistas of influence are opened, boundless possibilities of bringing happiness to those around us whose environment we so largely form. Throughout the " Mill on the Floss "—a history understood to be, as regards the mental experience of the heroine, in great part an autobiography—we find traced with almost passionate insistence the misery of a young life cast in uncongenial surroundings and wrestling with a hunger for unattainable joys of sense, of knowledge, of emotion. Who can read the sorrowful record of unsatisfied yearning, unbroken save by the yet darker shadow of a hope whose fruition was but sacrifice, without a sense of quickened sympathy with all noble souls groaning under the bonds of circumstance, of more ardent resolve to do his part in " widening the skirts of light and making the struggle with darkness narrower ? "

> "There is no hopelessness so sad as that of early youth, when the soul is made up of wants. . . . Maggie was a creature full of eager and passionate longing for all that was beautiful and glad; thirsty for all knowledge; with an ear straining after dreamy music that died away, and would not come near to her; with a blind unconscious yearning for something that would link together the wonderful impressions of this mysterious life, and give her soul a sense of home in it."—*Mill on the Floss*, i. 368-9.

But a still higher note is struck in the lament over Dorothea's failure to realise her wide and lofty aims for the welfare of others. If the purest of the egoistic impulses, desire of truth, love of beauty, effort after a wider sphere of energy, may fail of fruition from want of fit surroundings, still more are the altruistic affections, in which the life of humanity finds its ultimate satisfaction, likely to outrun the development of the conditions in which alone their exercise is possible.

> "Many Theresas have been born who found for themselves no epic life wherein there was a constant unfolding of far-resonant action; perhaps only a life of mistakes, the offspring of a certain spiritual grandeur, ill-matched with the meanness of opportunity. . . . With dim lights and tangled circumstances they tried to shape their thought and deed in noble agreement; but after all to common eyes their struggles seemed mere inconsistency and formlessness; for these later-born Theresas were helped by no coherent social faith which could perform the function of knowledge for the ardently willing soul."—*Middlemarch*, i. 2.

In this dissonance lies the deepest tragedy of human life, the least open to remedy by individual effort. Each step in pursuit of a higher ideal widens the range of possible divergence of interest. The pioneers are borne by the current of their own disinterestedness out of reach of the sympathy which is their life. The triumphal car of progress crushes its victims with relentless force.

We come now to George Eliot's view of religion. The keynote may be found in her definition of religion as consisting of the "feelings developed by the knowledge of the irreversible laws within and without." The theory of life definite or indefinite, which each of us holds, has its dynamic counterpart in the corresponding synthesis of action. Our philosophy and our conduct are but different aspects of a single relation—the relation between the inner and outer forces. Emotion, it has been already said, is the subjective correlate of action; conduct is generalised action; the generalised expression of emotion is religion. It is this recognition of the subjective nature of religion, and the relative character of its theoretical foundation—varying as it does with every advance in evolution—that lies at the root of George Eliot's sympathetic attitude towards all forms of faith. Widely different creeds are bound together in an estimate of their significance which discerns, underlying their conflicting claims to absolute authority, the substantial identity of the emotions they symbolise.

"The life-currents that ebb and flow in human hearts, pulsate to the same great needs, the same great loves and terrors. . . . We are impressed with the broad sameness of the human lot, which never alters in the main headings of its history—hunger and labour, seed-time and harvest, love and death."—*Romola*, i. 2.

In her portrayal of such types as Dinah Morris, Savonarola, Rufus Lyon, Mordecai, whose zeal rests on a comparatively narrow doctrinal basis, she expresses no less real an appreciation of the essence of religious feeling common to all, than in relation to phases of thought more nearly allied to her own intellectual position. We have here but another aspect of the historical standpoint to which are due the conceptions, already referred to, of the solidarity of the human race and the continuity of its development from simpler forms of life. The scientific spirit demands that the explanation of every phenomenon shall be sought in an account of its genesis; religion, like the other facts of our nature, is understood only by studying its origin and history. Let us consider some of the results of this method as shown in George Eliot's attitude towards the leading religious beliefs now current. What has she to tell us of the soul, of God, of a future life? Have these any place in the new synthesis?

Intellectual evolution may almost be defined as the process of distinguishing the objective from the subjective. Our own actions have both aspects. We feel while we act, and by combining the evidence of the senses we may also regard ourselves as external objects. But individual actions cannot be viewed as detached from their surroundings. We recognise ourselves as their *cause*, by which term we crudely express the fact that the direction of organic force is determined by the sum of preceding conditions—the *ensemble* of functions in course of co-ordination, which in its conscious or subjective aspect constitutes personality or *soul*. Out of our experience of those phenomena, which we refer to ourselves, there is thus established in our minds an association between a manifestation of force and such a group of organic conditions as appears to our consciousness; and it is assumed that this principle of explanation may be universally applied. The forces of the environment are, like our own actions, referred to a *personal cause*.

Such an extension of the primitive method of philosophising is largely justified by the confirmation it receives in the actions of the other organisms, whose energy forms so great a proportion of external forces, and whose communicated experiences harmonise with our own. All the more confidently is the principle carried into the remaining element of the environment, the sphere of *inorganic* forces, but here no similar evidence confirms it, and the gradual discovery of its inapplicability, and the substitution of an objective method, sum up the whole history of scientific philosophy.

The course of subjective explanation starts from a

fetishistic phase where every natural object is endowed with personality, and culminates in a monotheistic belief which generalises the antecedents of all phenomena in the conception of God as a personal first cause of the universe. Meanwhile, the scientific process of classifying facts without reference to hypothetical causes, basing its claim to acceptance on its more accurate prevision of the future, has been gradually supplanting the more *naïve* interpretation. The history of the struggle is a record of concessions made to the new method. The personal character of the deity gradually disappears; the sphere of his action is narrowed by each fresh objective generalisation; one class of facts after another becomes entirely emancipated from theological influence, and 'the whole conception is finally merged in a vague pantheism which makes its peace with the new synthesis in the guise of a psychological artifice—a convenience of language for the expression of a subjective unity which has no counterpart in objective reality.

The evolution thus traced in its intellectual aspect may be looked at also from the practical side.

"Religion can only change when the emotions that fill it are changed."—*Middlemarch*, iii. 134.

It has been already pointed out that thought, feeling, and action are really one. Structure and function cannot be separated; an addition to our knowledge, a change in our belief, means sooner or later a change in our life. Cause and effect cannot well be distinguished; action and reaction are equal. But the initiative seems to alternate, and we may now look on the other side. Emotion is the accompaniment of action, complete or incipient, and forms an index of its influence on thought. Let us follow the evolution of religious feeling, and note its reaction on the relative conceptions.

In primitive stages of development, the external forces surrounding each organism are, for the most part, antagonistic. Other organisms prey on it; dangers lie on every side. Nature is sparing of her gifts, and the struggle for existence is severe. The consciousness of individual helplessness, of action under outward constraint is the most persistent, and the personalities to which the external forces are referred, are conceived as beings of malignant power. This is the religion of fear. But man slowly learns to cope with nature; family and social ties supersede relations of general enmity; the secrets of life are gradually surrendered. Action is no less rigorously determined from without, but the environment is moulding the organism in harmony with itself, and the sense of opposition is disappearing. God has become beneficent; *fear* changes its character and becomes *reverence*.

But the more intimate knowledge of the true nature of our surroundings brings to light the predominance of the social factor. The growing sympathy with our fellow-creatures, to the influence of which such a change of feeling towards God is largely due, comes to demand a more concrete and more definitely-known object. A compromise of conceptions was effected in the Christian doctrine of the Incarnation. "God was made man;" or, in more modern phrase, *Man was made God.* Round the person of Jesus were gathered the emotions of both orders, and theism acquired a new lease of life in its coalescence with the idealisation of humanity. But the compromise could be only temporary; it fell short of complete truth, and its inadequacy was felt not less on the intellectual than on the emotional side. The Divine element in religion has now but a formal place; it is theoretically retained as a sanction to more vital emotions. The only persistent religious principle is the law of brotherly love, of universal sympathy, which forms the common watchword of all our systems, and which finds a wider reach and a fuller doctrinal expression in the Positivist generalisation of all human ideals. The transference of religious feeling from an object of subjective conception to one of definite knowledge and natural relationship, and its corresponding change of character from an abject fear to a "perfect love which casteth out fear," is thus seen to form an intelligible phase of organic development, the study of which leads us to a standpoint from which we may regard the negativism of the Agnostic as due to an imperfect psychological and historical analysis, while we condemn as shallow and unscientific the crude dogmatism of the Materialist who says not only in his heart but on the house-tops, "There is no God."

It is not of course suggested that any such formulation of the above theory is to be found in the pages of George Eliot. As an artist, she cannot represent complex intellectual processes; her creations can only embody the resulting beliefs. Her adherence to the above explanation of the history of theistic ideas may be recognised apart from external evidence by a combined view of her appreciative treatment of all phases of religious doctrine, and the various indications throughout her works of her personal feeling that all such subjective modes of thought are at their best only relatively valuable and transitional in nature.

An expression of this feeling is found in her reference to the

> "Rarer, better, truer, self,
> That sobbed religiously in yearning song,
> That watched to ease the burthen of the world:
> Laboriously tracing what must be
> And what may yet be better—saw within
> A worthier image for the sanctuary,
> And shaped it forth before the multitude,
> Divinely human, raising worship so,
> To higher reverence more mixed with love."—*Poems*, p. 301.

Her view of immortality follows naturally from the above conception. The reality of the spiritual world, far from being questioned or ignored in her writings, is emphasized, but again a more refined and subtle interpretation is offered in place of the primitive aspect of the truth. The spiritual life in its widest sense is shown to be identical with the world of thoughts and feelings which forms the inner side of organic experience. The soul may be defined as an abstract expression of individual life in its subjective aspect. The notion of its being a separate entity, distinct from the body, has obtained sanction from the possibility of separating in thought the two classes of phenomena, which a more careful analysis proves to be essentially identical and to differ only in aspect. The conception of a continued existence for the soul after the death of the body, will come to be regarded as no more reasonable than that of a shield of which one side remains while the other is destroyed.

But the hope of immortality feeds not less on belief than on desire; the wish is father to the thought. The increase of opportunity for the exercise of our powers, which accompanies the adaptation of structure to environment, affords experiences which give birth to the conviction that all our persistent desires will in one way or another certainly find satisfaction. A principle which is in the ascendant is apt to be cavalier in its treatment of opposing evidence. The facts, too obtrusive to be disregarded, which negatived such a confident optimism, were accorded only a superficial significance, the final issues being referred to an ideal sphere where poetic justice should overrule the anomalies of terrestial fate. The miseries of this life, pain and sorrow, unsatisfied longing, broken ties—all formed but fresh arguments for the existence of a world to come. The less of a heaven there is now, the more certainly must there be one hereafter.

Is this hope nothing but a vain imagination? Does scientific philosophy allow no belief in a wider scope for individual life than is bounded by the cradle and the grave? There *is* a reality which such visions forecast. We are no creatures of a day; our life is bound alike to the past and to the future by indissoluble ties. In a truer sense than the poet thought of,

> "The soul that rises with us, our life's star
> Hath had elsewhere its setting,
> And cometh from afar."

The ancestral life which beats in us will afterwards animate our children, and in a broader if less direct line, we inherit and may gather into our being the countless treasures of experience which past generations bequeath to us, while we in our turn transmit to all succeeding ages the influences we impress on the common life of humanity. The doctrine of subjective immortality finds its highest expression in the poem of George Eliot's, from which a passage has been already quoted:—

"Oh may I join the choir invisible
Of those immortal dead who live again
In minds made better by their presence; live
In pulses stirred to generosity,
In deeds of daring rectitude, of scorn
For miserable aims that end with self,
In thoughts sublime that pierce the night like stars,
And with their mild persistence urge men's souls
To vaster issues . . . .

. . . This is life to come
Which martyred men have made more glorious
For us who strive to follow. May I reach
That purest heaven, be to other souls
The cup of strength in some great agony,
Enkindle generous ardour, feed pure love,
Beget the smiles that have no cruelty,
Be the sweet presence of a good diffused,
And in diffusion ever more intense :
So shall I join the choir invisible,
Whose music is the gladness of the world."—*Poems*, p. 301.

But the reply comes from many lips—" We know all this, but it is not enough. We ask for bread, and you give us a stone. Our wish is for a *personal* immortality, a continuance of consciousness beyond the limit of a scant threescore years and ten. Take this hope from us, and life becomes a vain show without aim or interest, a riddle which we cannot read."

Very many of those who would instinctively make this reply are deceiving themselves in their estimate of their present need for such a belief. They are better than they think. They would not cease to work and love, to pity and help while yet it was day, however dark a night they feared. To those who really feel as they say, the only answer is—My friends, you do *not* " know all this ; " or you know it only in the sense of no longer venturing to deny it. It has not entered into your soul; it is not a part of your being. You ask eternal life; but what is life? Is it not the full and harmonious exercise of all powers and faculties, the development of which is justified by surrounding conditions? The primary egoistic functions which constitute physical vigour will always demand due exercise during the term of bodily strength, and recoil from the suggestions of sudden interruption conveyed in every sensation of pain and every instance of untimely death. But when such exercise is secured by the growing immunity from accident and disease which accompanies progression in knowledge,—when death ceases to come prematurely, and coincides with the limit of natural decay, there will then remain no claim for prolonged existence from this side of our nature. When men enjoy earthly life to the full, they will no longer be unwilling to die.

"But what consolation," it is asked, "does a vision of universal euthanasia for remote posterity bring to us with whom death makes no terms? His sting pierces young and old around us; the victory of the grave is proclaimed on every side."

The hardship is real, but not without remedy. In the night of death there is no darkness equal to the shadow which it casts before it. The "happy dead" know nothing of unfulfilled desire; it is the present fear which has begot the doctrine of personal immortality, and this fear is the reflex of an unrestrained egoism, the continuance of which is not sanctioned by the ultimate conditions of existence. Already, in the highest phases of evolution at least, the altruistic tendencies are dominant, and their persistent encroachment on the sphere of lower impulses involves a reconstruction of the ideal of life. The fear of death is slowly being expelled by the sympathetic affections which preoccupy the mind. These are the functions which promise to form the ruling element in human nature, and it is their exercise which must first be considered in the final conception of an after-life. The less of self-seeking, the more love and thought for others, there is in our conduct, the less eager will be our concern for our personal interests in an indefinite future. When we have ceased to long for such an immortality, we shall find that we have unconsciously ceased to believe in it; the prize of our deepest and noblest aspirations will consist in the sure knowledge of the place that awaits us in the "choir invisible, whose music makes the gladness of the world."

Such are the creed and teaching of George Eliot. We have tried to show that her artistic work draws its inspiration from intellectual materials which have been welded together in a wider synthesis than any previous system has attained—a synthesis in which the deepest problems of human life, the nature of duty, of happiness, of sympathy, of the soul, of God, of immortality, are interpreted and unified by a common reference to ascertained scientific law. It is claimed that such a philosophy is an advance on preceding positions in the line of evolution, not only as representing a closer correspondence between knowledge and outward reality, between thought and things, but also on the ground of affording a greater freedom to action and emotion.

Though the confidence of its anticipations based on the past history of progress is qualified by a knowledge of the limitations of evolution—the ever-present possibility of degeneracy and dissolution on the one hand,

and the still more insidious dangers of individual and social parasitism on the other, it is nevertheless substantially an optimistic faith. How then shall we explain the undercurrent of sadness with which it is here presented to us in the pages of one of its chief exponents, and which often forms an argument for an impeachment of its truth? The answer is threefold.

To begin with, the more consistent effort after scientific accuracy of conception does not attain its end without a sacrifice of attractiveness. A religion which satisfies the demands of reality by an arbitrary separation of human destinies into two diverging streams, opposing to its apparent balance of unlimited optimism a formal exaggeration of the other side of the account, has greater charms—meretricious though they be—for those whose consciousness of merit exceeds their power of reflection, and to such it will continue to appeal with more persuasive force than is at the command of a faith which dares to countenance no hopes but those warranted by well-attested facts.

The second part of the answer is suggested by George Eliot's own words, in her reference to "the suffering, whether of martyr or victim, which belongs to every historical advance of mankind." Happiness, it has been seen, is the correlate of such action only as is in harmony with the environment—a category which excludes action in course of adjustment to a new ideal. The intellectual evolution which is the measure of such a change can reach its fruition in the unfolding of a more perfect life, only at the cost of preliminary pain. When a new equilibrium has been established, the natural relation of conduct and emotion will be restored.

The remaining cause of George Eliot's melancholy

is more personal. She is an artist, and to be an artist is to be conservative. We have in her an instance of a nature in a sense divided against itself, seeking the satisfaction of its artistic powers, where alone it can be found, in aspects of life which represent a relation of the inner and outer forces sufficiently settled to admit of the free play of emotion, and at the same time finding its intellectual affinities in a system of thought which is still far from being an organic possession of the human race. It is the union of a sentiment which loves to linger in the past, and a keen vision that pierces the veil of the future, that brings some slight sense of discord into a mind otherwise serene, but it is in the very uniqueness of such a position that much of her deepest influence lies. Such influence, may be, as yet, limited in sphere, but its power is great in those whom it reaches. Her martyrdom has not been in vain, and no crown could be more precious to her than to be "the cup of strength" to the workers whose lives are devoted to the advancement of the truths she delighted to honour.

But we claim for her a higher place than this. The greatest artistic work, we are told, is that which is in harmony with contemporary life and thought. If the artist prefer like Landor to "dine late" with "guests few and select," the wish is taken for a confession of failure. But the court of judgment must vary with the changing conditions of mental development. With ever-increasing differences in the possibilities of culture, the range of sympathetic appeal becomes ever narrower in the sphere of its immediate influence, with a compensatory extension at some later time. Shakespeare could write for the many of his own day, and for all succeeding ages; the artist of the present must be content to appeal to the few of his own generation, and the many of the generations that are to come.

The influence of George Eliot will widen as we approach the goal of her aspirations.

"Even as in music, where all obey and concur to one end, so that each has the joy of contributing to a whole, whereby he is ravished and lifted up into the court of heaven, so will it be in that crowning time of the millennial reign, when our daily prayer will be fulfilled, and one law shall be written on all hearts, and be the very structure of all thought, and be the principle of all action."

III.

JOHN RUSKIN

ECONOMIST

OF old sang Chaucer of the Flower and Leaf,
 The mirthful singer of a golden time;
 And sweet birds' song throughout his daisied rhyme
Rang fearless; for our cities held no grief
 Dumb in their blackened hearts beneath the grime
Of factory and furnace, and the sheaf
 Was borne in gladness at the harvest-time.
So now the Seer would quicken our belief:
 'Life the green leaf,' saith he, 'and Art the flower:
Blow, winds of heaven, about the hearts of men,
 Come love, and hope, and helpfulness, as when
On fainting vineyard falls the freshening shower;
 Fear not that life may blossom yet again,
A nobler beauty from a purer power!'

JOHN RUSKIN.

THE surprise, perplexity, and sometimes indeed exasperation with which so many of even the more sympathetic of Mr. Ruskin's earlier readers and critics have received his recent works must be frankly admitted, and as far as possible accounted for. To most people, ordinary difficulties, such as are exhibited by other authors, whether of unconventionality of thought, profundity of learning, or intricacy of style, are far exceeded by the personal one—of interpreting what seems an unreasonable and violent change of career. They hear of a veteran art teacher, critic, and man of letters suddenly casting aside his hard-won laurels, resuming the weapons with which in his youth he had hardly slain the small art-critics of the magazines, dashing off into apparently the most remote of all possible fields, that of political economy, casting down his glove in challenge among its sturdy and sober cultivators, loudly proclaiming their patiently-gathered harvest mere tares and darnel, hurling blazing pamphlets into the overflowing granaries of their science, and charging with fiery impetuosity against its massive logic mills.

It is not, then, to be wondered at, if the bystanders, mostly plain common-sense people, who think that art and political economy are no doubt all very well, but will get on best, as they themselves have done, by minding their own business and letting that of other folks alone, see in this would-be-delivering knight only the latest avatar of the truly immortal hero of Cervantes, and so either join merrily in the hooting, or pass by in sorrow, as their own moral temper happens to incline. Even from those who love progress so warmly as not to be deterred by the strange appearance of the new reformer, and who seek the out-of-the-way village where costly books are published for poor men, we gather tidings of the establishment for the hundredth time of a new Utopia,—surely at most an ominous sign that the leaven of economic heresy, which is spreading so fast on the Continent and in America, and with such grim results of Socialism and Communism, of Nihilism and Anarchy, is in our quiet industrial community too, and will henceforth work. The student, indeed, who has learned from Bismarck, Hildebrand, or Lassalle, statesman, professor, and radical alike, that our German neighbours are bent upon giving Socialism a trial, and are only delayed by the discussion of comparative details, may read on in hopes of some luminous suggestions; but what is to be learned or hoped from a man who speaks contemptuously of all the highest practical achievements of the nineteenth century? For him is not its science either of mere mechanism or evolutionary nonsense; its physics and mathematics mere aids to railroad and telegraph making; its chemistry and biology mere disgusting curiosity about stinks and bones;—its splendid development of modern commerce and finance is little better than complex thieving; the steam engine is a filthy nuisance, never to set wheel on St. George's lands; our vast and prosperous industrial cities are so many working models of hell; nay, even our hard-won system of education with its clear practical aims is to make way for schools with a curriculum of Latin, and botany, and the history of Florence! Here, surely, we have a clue to the right critical estimate. Our would-be economist is but an artist born out of his proper mediæval time; his mournful jeremiads, nay, whole books of lamentations, with their wailing retrospects of the good old times, and their bitterly pessimist prophecies, far out-Carlyling Carlyle, are perhaps natural for him, but clearly useless for us; so let us either take what amuses us in the art books, say the scenery in "Modern Painters," to which considerable merit of style is undeniable, or if we find even that as well done in novels now-a-days, let him alone altogether.

Such is, probably, a fair statement of the opinions to which a very large number of the reading public have steadily settled down: a minority, however, still dissent more or less completely from this estimate, and appeal for a new reading, apparently in confident hope of ultimately obtaining a less unfavourable judgment. Deceived though the latter class may be by mere rhetorical finish and sentimental glow, we cannot, in the interest of fair play, refuse to give them a new hearing, or to briefly re-examine for ourselves the economic position of Mr. Ruskin, and that of the orthodox English economist, who is the more especial object of his attacks. But let it be clearly understood that the writer is no grateful art-student, if such there be; still less any enthusiastic Guildsman of St. George, eager to do battle for his master; but a quiet student of science and economics, one of those scholars of Huxley and Darwin, of Spencer and Comte, of whom

Mr. Ruskin has so often spoken other than smooth things. One aim, however, is clearly avowed—an aim characteristic of all the essays of the present series—that of attempting to substitute the scientific for the literary method of criticism. The ordinary journalistic method of criticising a book like Mr. Ruskin's " Fors Clavigera," namely, that of quoting only some web of paradox or burst of passion, is at once dishonest to the author and misleading to the reader. The scientific attitude should be the precise reverse of this. The student, if genuinely trained at all, soon lays aside the slim text-book which incompletely summarizes the facts of his science from one author's own narrow standpoint, and learns to work his way dispassionately through the vast literature which lies behind it; often wearily wading through shallow seas of verbiage, or toiling patiently through deserts of details, useless and numberless as the sand; now silently evading some dismal swamp of error, often crushing a whole stony volume for a few grains of genuine gold. Nuggets indeed there are, but never gold-beds nor Aladdin palaces, and even the traveller's own hard-won treasure will need refining and re-refining by his intellectual heirs. So then if we agree to take up the scientific attitude, if, instead of collecting curiosities of apparent or real error leaving the truth behind, we seek to gather out of these masses of new and strange thought whatever we find, on fair analysis, to be true metal, we are ready to begin gold washing.

But, before making any further analysis of our heretical economist, we must obtain some basis of comparison and ascertain something of the orthodox ones, whom (disregarding of course their many minor differences), we may take as fairly represented in the domain of practical life by statesmen like Lord Sherbrooke, John Bright, or the Duke of Argyll; or again, by the majority of the economic professoriate of Britain, among whom it is hardly necessary to recall such distinguished names as Stanley Jevons or Sidgwick, Bonamy Price or Hodgson, Fawcett or Levi. Here, surely, is a school of thinkers of whom our country may be justly proud, men of high education and honourable aims, who have not only brought to the investigation of their subject an intellectual subtlety and force unsurpassed by the students of any science, and to its exposition a calm logical clearness and precision which their colleagues in university or senate might, for the most part, well envy, but, when opportunity for practical action has been given them, have often seemed to unite the best qualities of industrialist and theorician, of statesman and philanthropist.

This, then, we may surely regard as an ideal scientific school, that may well claim to take rank with those of geology or biology, medicine or engineering, which have been doing such splendid work during the last generation. Many fully allow this claim, many perhaps ignore; yet to its full recognition one difficulty alone arises, which, though seemingly of small importance alike to the economist and to the public, is serious enough from our present scientific standpoint to need brief examination.

Without going over all the stages by which the place of economics among the sciences has been defined by philosophers, the reader may be reminded that logic and mathematics, dealing with the abstract relations of quality and quantity, underlie and precede the physical, natural, and social sciences; that of these physics and chemistry are antecedent to the strictly biological group (which includes zoology, botany, physiology, etc), while the social sciences, having for their subject the phenomena presented by those organisms, which, like bees and ants, beavers and men, live in communities, are obviously founded upon the whole preceding mass of knowledge, which is accordingly grouped under the convenient title of "Preliminary Sciences." In other words, the successful treatment of the social science requires not merely a discipline in mathematics, as some suppose, still less mere training in academic metaphysic and dialectic—which is all that so many bring to the task—but some sound knowledge of living beings and of the physical laws to which they are subject.

While the details of this classification of the sciences are, among philosophers, the subject of a dispute—happily of no consequence here,—it is accepted for all essential practical purposes, alike in the organisation of learned societies and in the scientific curriculum of universities, that is to say, in the actual teaching and learning of the world. Now the difficulty in fully recognising the British economists as scientific lies in the existence, during the past generation, if not indeed during the entire century, of the most complete state of war between the economists on the one hand, and the cultivators of the preliminary sciences on the other. This is evidenced not merely by the almost complete suspension of relations between the two camps, or by the fact that only here and there a scientific society accepts economic communications, but also by the frequent occurrence of positive battle. A convenient recent instance of this is afforded by the history of what is after all our most representative scientific parliament—the British Association. This body divides its labours broadly in accordance with the classification of the sciences above referred to into sections, respectively entitled—(*a*) Mathematics and physics; (*b*) chemistry; (*c*) geology; (*d*) biology (including anthropology); (*e*) economics and statistics, together with (*f*) geography, and (*g*) mechanical science; the former being separated from geology for convenience sake, and the latter being exclusively concerned with the practical applications of science.

The scientific sections of the British Association are well known to be much less sternly scientific than the respective special societies, while the economic section, on the other hand, bears a decidedly more serious and thorough character than kindred bodies, such as the Social Science Congress. Yet so little have the students of the preliminary sciences respected the discussions of their economic brethren, that their dissatisfaction culminated, in 1876, in an active attempt to excommunicate the latter, to cut off the Economic Section, root and branch, as no better than a disgrace to a scientific association. (This almost total failure of the section to accomplish any scientific work was avowed with the most startling frankness by its president, Mr. Grant Duff, in an opening address at the jubilee meeting of the Association in 1881, which is worth reading, as being pretty certainly the least jubilant historical retrospect ever made by any learned body whatever). To avert an expulsion, which would have so grievously discredited political economy in the public eye, the section sought an apologist, and wisely selected Mr. Ingram of Dublin as its president for 1878. Mr. Ingram delivered a masterly address, which, in Mr. Grant Duff's retrospect, is rightly described as "the most elaborate and brilliant to which the section had ever listened." In this essay, soon widely circulated throughout Europe, "On the Present Position and Prospects of Political Economy," although appointed to bless his economic brethren, he well-nigh cursed them altogether, at once pleading guilty for them to all the accusations of their scientific assailants, and delivering a destructive criticism of the past and present of British economics—a criticism exceeding anything of that kind ever attempted by Mr. Ruskin, as much in completeness as in calm. By as ably vindicating, however, the claims of sociology to its supreme place among the sciences, as by proposing complete reforms, the attack upon the Economic Section was skilfully averted, and it remains yet awhile in hope of better fruit. Finally, three years later, at the mournful jubilee above referred to, Mr. Grant Duff, from the presidential chair, repeated, extended, and enforced, all the criticisms and proposals of Ingram, without a word of protest or even deprecation. If, then, we can ascertain precisely what the defects of our orthodox economists, as now exposed and admitted, really are, we shall immediately be able to examine not only Mr. Ruskin's heresies, but all other cases of dissent, from a new stand-point, and by clearer light.

Political economy has often been popularly nicknamed "the dismal science," but nothing can really be more striking than the cheerful optimism of our orthodox economist, who often gives, as Cairnes puts it, "a handsome ratification of the existing state of society as approximately perfect," for is it not determined by "immutable law"? and has not Adam Smith established the harmony of a community under "enlightened self-interest?" What could be more modern and scientific than this conception of harmonious law? Yet not so; German economists have clearly shewn how the "Wealth of Nations" is no pure economic treatise, but subtly permeated, though the matter-of-fact British reader may not notice it, with all the philosophy of its author's day. This beautiful harmony of interests, in short, has nothing in common with our grim modern doctrine of the "Struggle for Existence;" it is identical with the early teleological view which Darwin has expelled from biology; it is the modern survival of Leibnitz's "Pre-established Harmony," and the exponent of this as the "best of all possible worlds" turns out to be the Dr. Pangloss, of "Candide." But the worthy theologian has suffered so sorely at the hands of all his critics that he dares only venture to assert "this is the best of all possible worlds" from the economic rostrum.

This certainly is not encouraging, but we must not let a trifling criticism of this sort prejudice us against the economist; we shall surely find him sound and scientific in the main points of his science. What, then, is its fundamental conception? "Utility," answers Mr. Jevons; "wealth," says Mr. Mill; and these two definitions come to the same thing, for wealth consists of "utilities fixed and embodied in permanent objects." What surely can seem more practical and more scientific than this conception of utility? What trace of obsolete philosophy can linger here? Alas! strange as it may seem, the whole spirit of mediæval metaphysics. This utility, this central idea of the economic "science," has nothing whatever to do with science, and, whether in the hands of Bentham or Mill, Jevons or Sherbrooke, it matters not, is essentially a figment of antique scholasticism for all!

For, observe, the conception of utility corresponds

exactly to that of vitality in biology; just as wealth is utility fixed or embodied in permanent objects, so of course organisms were long defined as vitalities fixed and embodied in permanent objects. But the biologist without any more doubting that organisms are alive than that wealth is useful has long utterly scorned, and, what is better, utterly abandoned the attempt to make his science the study of vitality. While his grandfather, the last century physician, commenced with definitions of vitality, and talked much of animal spirits, of humours and the like, he observes each organism in its past and present relations in actual space and time, analyses its structures, and inquires how they work, generalises his observations, and then is done. The old apothecary, too, explained that opium made one sleep in virtue of its inherent dormitiveness ("*virtus dormitiva*"), but, thanks to Molière, the profession has since learned that the fixture and embodiment of an entity called dormitiveness into the permanent object opium does not explain anything, much less form the basis of a science of therapeutics: the physician now simply observes and applies the fact, and when asked why application of this curious mixture of alkaloids should have this particular effect frankly avows his ignorance, and sets about experimenting.

So, too, the physicist, when he observes that water only rises thirty-two feet in his pump, no longer appeals to the "natural law" by which "nature abhors a vacuum;" he no longer explains the regular movements of a watch by reference to its "horologity" or of a jack by help of "an inherent meat-roasting principle." The physicist and naturalist may well be surprised to learn that the dormitiveness of opium and the horology of clocks, so far from having wholly disappeared from modern thought into the history of its emancipation, have actually been generalised into a new entity—"*utility*," and thus form the subject of an inquiry, which its cultivators, indeed, describe as a "hypothetical" or as an "abstract science," but which, we see, requires the addition of the prefix "pseudo—," or the affix "falsely so called," for its more accurate definition.

If space allowed, it would be easy to show how this vicious tendency to invent abstractions instead of working out generalisations, runs through the whole subject. Thus the quantity of anything which happens to be demanded, and the supply which happens to be forthcoming, at a given place and time, are legitimate and profitable objects for statistical and historical research. These, the two real aspects of the subject, however, are generally neglected, and by the simpler process of spelling with capitals, "Supply and Demand" become raised into the mysterious regulators of society by means of "inexorable laws," and are thus, since things which are equal to the same thing are equal to one another, practically identical with the "Fate," "Kismet," and "Providence" of Pagan, Mohammedan, and Christian philosophers. Nor is the logic less quaintly interesting than the metaphysics. The endless initial squabbles about definitions, the old disputes whether the inductive or deductive method alone is to be used, as reasonable as if naturalists were to quarrel at the outset of their studies whether eyes were to be bandaged or hands tied, might all detain us. One favourite practice we may conveniently describe as "generalisation of the incongruous." The absurdity of the jumbling of material things A B C, with immaterial things $x\,y\,z$,—intentional in such well-known lines as "Brimful of wrath and cabbage," "They sought it with forks and hope,"—is concealed alike from author and readers, by first uniting them under some vague general term of common language, such as Capital, and then subjecting this to an elaborate analysis, setting up a new series of abstract entities $L\,M\,N$, such as fixed capital, circulating capital, and what not, in which the original realities are all hopelessly confused; finally treating this by an apparatus of metaphor, which, because far more elaborate and recondite—but, it must be confessed, considerably less imaginative—than that of poetry, requires a deceptive resemblance to scientific comparison in sober prose. The quaint and comparatively intelligible phrases of the newspapers, such as "tallow is firm," "pig iron lively," are not taken for anything more than the poetry of 'Change: Mr. Fawcett, however, apparently supposes himself to have enunciated a scientific conception, when he explains that "the remuneration of capital is the reward of abstinence." The expression "clotted nonsense" has been thought scarcely admissible in literary criticism, but the definition of capital as "thickly curdled working time," has appeared to some economists profoundly scientific.

If we now enter upon the actual examination of economic literature, we find our apparently homogeneous science breaking up into innumerable discordant schools. While the legal and literary economists, like those of the school of Ricardo, imagine that by adroitly spinning and weaving definitions and syllogisms in their logic mills, they manufacture a body of "natural laws" thereafter rigid and universal as those of mathematics, the economist of mathematical turn, like Gabaglio or Jevons, proclaims the potency of the "statistical method," or maintains that algebra and the calculus furnish the true means of economic investigation. To such minds, the theory of exchange seems of course fundamental, but the economist of more practical and physical turn devotes himself especially to the study of "material wealth, its production, distribution, and consumption," while both classes often stoutly refuse consideration to the nature and wants of the community for and by whom this wealth is produced and consumed. The majority of economists, however, having had their attention drawn to the rate of reproduction in organic beings by Malthus, become in so far biologists. Yet nothing more effectually demonstrates the extraordinary slenderness of their scientific pretensions than that their physical discussions are heedless of the very existence of the modern doctrine of energy (if indeed they do not involve some contradiction of its fundamental law), or that "competition" and the "laws of population" are discussed without an apparent suspicion that Malthus' own clue has led, in the hands of Darwin, to the construction of a vast theory which has revolutionised not only modern biology, and with it our views of the origin, nature, and destiny of man, but shed brilliant light on all the other sciences which concern him. Lawyer and theologian, even poet and romancer, have been carried far by this tidal wave of thought, strong as that of the Revolution or the Renaissance; the economist alone remains behind, and though here, by exception, provided with some genuine though fragmentary scientific conceptions of evolution and the struggle for existence, he delays to modernise them by the aid of the new learning, supposing, doubtless, that even these—"progress," "competition," "co-operation," and the like, are sacred metaphysical abstractions too.

It is needless for the economist to reply with Mr. Fawcett, that "these do not come within his province," or with Mr. Bonamy Price, that "he cannot hope to become a specialist." The naturalist has long ago discerned and proclaimed that the phenomena of human society are as dependent upon biology as those of ant or bee society, and the orthodox economist must either straightway follow the example of the students of mind and language, whose (then unreformed) studies not so long ago seemed equally remote from those humble microscopic inquiries to which they likewise supposed the biologist to be confined, and either adopt and apply the conceptions of modern physics and biology, or disappear in the unavailing struggle for existence against them. For ever since the constitution of sociology upon the preliminary sciences by Comte half a century ago, the result has been certain. Spencer and his school have continued the siege, and signs of all kinds from both sides that the war is well nigh over are not wanting. On the side of the besieged economists, the more far-sighted leaders, like Mr. Ingram and Mr. Grant Duff, are unconditionally surrendering the citadel, and indeed taking arms on the side of the invaders; while among the latter, Huxley or Hæckel or Vogt can hardly write a zoological text-book without some jubilant prediction of the speedy conquest of the social sciences.

Is it attempted to stop the breach by appeal to mental or moral science? Archaic psychological and ethical conceptions—frequently of course of fundamental importance—are dragged up from the dusty

academic crypts, where they have escaped contact with
the ideas of the century, to be hurled at us, for have
they not supported the temple of economic orthodoxy
ever since Adam Smith (who had of course to work
with the crude notions of human nature and conduct
current in his day) sought to found economic and
moral sciences upon the irreconcilable and mutually
destructive assumptions of pure egoism and pure
altruism respectively, saying, let us found economics
on the notion of unrestrained self-interest, morals on
that of universal sympathy. In such "hypothetical
sciences," the hypothetical element is more evident
than the scientific; and these illusory simplifications of
the problem by denying the unity of nature and of
science need not detain us here, save that they are of
interest in accounting for those moving appeals against
emotion, and contemptuous dismissals of "sentiment"—
themselves choice examples of emotion and sentiment,
of course of the strictly egoistic or economic sort—
with which every reader of orthodox economic literature
is familiar. Nor, passing to the conceptions which
have so long done duty for social science, need even
the central myth of "Freedom of Contract," unrelated
as it is to anything known in modern sociology, detain
us farther than as it enables us to congratulate the pro-
jectors of the approaching centenary celebration of the
French Revolution, that five years hence some orthodox
economist will probably still survive to acknowledge
his indebtedness for the all important social assump-
tion of his hypothetical science, the "Contrat Social,"
to its illustrious author, that ingenious metaphysician
whom economists have never yet sufficiently honoured,
M. Jean Jacques Rousseau.

Enough, then, has probably been said to show that

these economists, even in so far as they claim to apply scientific conceptions at all, are unfortunately provided with curiously archaic and erroneous ones, and that their intellectual apparatus consists largely of broken down heirlooms, with which the attempt to work is what anthropologists call a "survival in culture."

If space allowed, it would be interesting to trace how, along with this preservation of false conceptions destroyed by science, and ignorance of true conceptions established by science, there is associated a marked scarcity of scientific observation and classification of phenomena, and a presence of that confusion of fact and hypothesis, of opinion and anecdote, of controversial trifling, and practical recipes of doubtful efficacy, which one only finds elsewhere in equal abundance in the scientific library of the middle ages. But the reader can easily go on tracing the close analogy between an orthodox "system of political economy" and a mediæval work on natural history, astrology, or alchemy, into its curious details; we have given perhaps too much time to this pursuit of intellectual palæontology. It would appear, then, that Mr. Ruskin (however he has come by it), has really had some considerable insight into this state of things, but unfortunately denounces it with the heat of an eager reformer instead of appreciating its high scientific interest, and describing it with the minuteness it deserves. For when every year are swarming down these hungry and all-devouring hordes of scientific invaders, whom neither spiritual nor temporal resistance can repel, whom neither the flapping of theologian's robes nor the wagging of lawyer's wigs can frighten from beginning to meddle with even their special business, and to whom the medical profession has deserted in a body, what is to become of the poor defenceless handful of metaphysicians who have so long had economics in their keeping? What is to become of optimism and pre-established harmony? The new-comers believe in what is a good deal like the reverse. What will become of the sacred entities? Providence - Supply - and - Demand will be blasphemed; utility and what not will go the way of *virtus dormitiva* and *vitality;* the "elementary conceptions of wealth, capital, labour," will be analysed as ruthlessly as the elements fire, air, earth, and water; that historic keystone of social order, the "Contrat Social" itself, will be exploded; every chapter of the hypothetical science will be punctured,—who—who will save us?

An as yet unknown aspect of "inexorable law" providentially interferes, which among the invaders will one day be known as Natural Selection. This goddess, more powerful and more beneficent than Supply-and-Demand, says :—

> Alas, my children, against the theologians you could indeed survive, and among the lawyers, the politicians, and the journalists, you were in the very camp of brethren, but these scientists are too strong for you; your doctrines and yourselves are doomed to inevitable extinction! Yet take courage, I will prolong your days many years: here is the secret! Acquire as fast as you can a deceptive external resemblance to the invaders; do not name your sacred dogmas as of old, but conceal the old matter under their newer manner; its aridity and difficulty will at once keep off the public, and impress them with profound reverence, while its superficial resemblance to science will long satisfy even the scientists, who have plenty to do yet awhile among their telescopes and balances, their fossils and their flowers. This do and live; you and your children shall go in and out under their very noses in safety; nay, you shall have 'scientific' societies of your own, even a whole department of the British Association all to yourselves, and though here and there

some impassioned socialist or quick-eyed art-critic may detect your true nature, nobody will believe them, it will be 1878 before you are properly dissected and classified, and I know not how long before you are finally extirpated. Fear not, therefore, this all-devouring march of science, become mimetic organisms in its ranks, and all shall long be well.

Now, behold, all these things have come to pass; and should any non-biological reader, or any orthodox economist, hitherto all unconscious of his ancient pedigree and modern family fortunes, desire to learn more of this gentle dispensation by which merciful nature often works such marvellous outward transformations, so softening the swift and stern extermination of an ancient species into its slow and painless euthanasia, is it not written by the naturalist Grant Allen, in the article "Mimicry" of the Encyclopædia Britannica, vol. xvi., Edinburgh, 1883?

But the reader must by this time be objecting, does not the preceding criticism overshoot its aim? Is it not too destructive and intolerant? Even if economists be unscientific, surely this comparison of political economy to alchemy is undeserved, else why were so many merits granted at the beginning? Now, however, our qualifications must be made. It would ill become the student of modern science to forget that to Roger Bacon the alchemist, and Kepler the astrologer, we owe priceless discoveries; it is only the persistence of alchemy or astrology as modern systems of doctrine that he would deprecate. So the scientific invaders of political economy must never forget in the excitement of victory that, while of its orthodox system hardly one stone can be left upon another, for new foundations have to be laid, the materials of the edifice and the treasures which its multifarious storehouses contained are abundant and precious enough to ransom the economists from any risk of disgrace or oblivion. Even in the ranks of the preliminary sciences advance is never simultaneous; one subject starts forward while another is lagging far behind; the mineralogist and chemist, the botanist and zoologist can never keep fairly abreast, even the new sociological economists are no whit exempt from the risk of fossilizing like their predecessors. What has been said, however, will clear the reader's mind of the error still common in England that our economists of Glasgow and Manchester, Edinburgh and London, have been erecting during the past century a vast scientific system of infallible dogma, around whose impregnable walls only our single " Oxford Graduate " wastes his arrows.

We have seen how the fortress is being stormed from a quite different side, nay, is already being sacked, for the scientific invaders are not respecters of persons, and will treat all who are not members of their own army with but scanty reverence, unceremoniously looting everything that will serve as materials for their new construction, whether they belonged to skilful financier or subtle logician, popular tribune or patrician senator, nay, will pay as little regard to the professor of political economy, robed in the spotless orthodoxy of the intellectual pharisee, as for his heterodox and despised publican of a colleague, the professor of fine art. The question for all is simply—What ideas have you that will serve as material for our purpose?

We saw at the outset how unfavourable a first impression of Mr. Ruskin's economic writings one was apt to acquire. The collapse of our plausible orthodox friends on closer examination, however, may warn us to be cautious in adhering to a prejudice which they or rather their exponents in the newspapers have done most to diffuse, and which he naturally incurred by loudly proclaiming, for so many years past, in season and out of season, the hollowness of their pseudo-science; so that whatever may turn out to be the value of the new doctrines he may offer us, his destructive criticisms, which have so long anticipated any scientific ones, such as that of Mr. Ingram or the present one, must accordingly on the whole be straightway transferred from the debit to the credit side of his account. Can any similar value be given to his criticisms of society? An explanation on the one side and a reservation on the other, both important, are first needed. Let us then read a complete typical passage:—

"What may be the real dignity of mechanical art itself? I cannot express the amazed awe, the crushed humility, with which I sometimes watch a locomotive take its breath at a railway station, and think what work there is in its bars and wheels, and what manner of men they must be who dig brown ironstone out of the ground, and forge it into that. What assemblage of accurate and mighty faculties in them, more than fleshly power over melting crag and coiling fire, fettered and finessed at last into the precision of watchmaking; Titanian hammer-strokes beating out of lava these glittering cylinders and timely respondent valves, and fine ribbed rods, which touch each other as a serpent writhes in noiseless gliding, and omnipotence of grasp; infinitely complex anatomy of active steel, compared with which the skeleton of a living creature would seem, to the careless observer, clumsy and vile. What would the men who thought out this, who beat it out, who touched it with its polished calm of power, who set it to its appointed task, and triumphantly saw it fulfil the task to the utmost of their will, feel or think about this weak hand of mine, timidly leading a little stain of water colour which I cannot manage, into an imperfect shadow of something else—mere failure in every motion and endless disappointment; what I repeat, would these iron-dominant genii think of me? and what ought I to think of them?

"But as I reach this point of reverence, the unreasonable thing is sure to give a shriek as of a thousand unanimous vultures, which leaves me shuddering in real physical pain for some half minute following; and assures me during slow recovery, that a people which can endure such fluting and piping among them is not likely soon to have its modest ear pleased by aught of oaten stop or pastoral song,".

The requisite correction, then, as afforded by the first paragraph of the present passage, is that the popular impression that our author abhors all machinery and recommends its disuse, and that he criticises all the material results and appliances of our modern civilisation in a similar spirit, is simply the reverse of true. For it will not be easy to find any panegyric of machines and their makers, though the age is rich in such literature, to match this, combining, as it does, the scientific appreciation of Babbage's classic "Economy of Machines and Manufactures," with the artistic appreciation which we find in the Surfaceman's "Songs of the Rail." In the second half of the passage, however, we find the grounds for the needful reservation; we discover that our prose poet of Utilitarianism suffers from acute hyperæsthesia, is, in other words, a man of excessively nervous organisation and evidently fragile health, upon whom those minor blessings of peculiar sights and sounds and smells, which do undoubtedly accompany and flow from our advanced mechanical civilisation, produce an effect serious in the extreme—he cannot become case-hardened to them like most of us.

Thus then arises the popular impression of Ruskin, quite analogous to that of the enraged musician in Hogarth's famous engraving. The young schoolboy in the picture naturally thinks "what fun to see the old boy so wild!" the disturbing crowd, offended at such interference, and all following their lawful callings, are equally astonished and naturally reply to all remonstrances with an indignant "what's your business!" and similarly the able editor, who has of course comfortably grown up in the orthodox economic faith, makes the most of this opportunity to damage its opponent, neatly snips out the proper fragment of a passage, exhibits our author in some attitude more passionate than dignified, and expounds the combined opinions of schoolboy and populace with due accustomed diluteness and detail.

Without in the least denying a certain justice to these criticisms, on the contrary bearing the personal equation with its results of misunderstanding, impatience, sometimes even positive ill-nature, henceforth in mind, may we not get beyond them? When we have had our laugh at the enraged musician, may we not stand quiet for a little to hear him play? All these noisy callings are lawful indeed, yet not perhaps expedient: some of them have disappeared since Hogarth's day, and we call it progress; in any case the musician's bitter outcry is not without its pathos and its truth. What worker in our dull towns, whether of country birth and breeding, or only accustomed to rare glimpses of hill and sea, is so completely acclimatised, so wholly dulled in vision, as never to suffer anything from the noise and darkness, the filth and grime around him? Surely, too, we must in the same measure feel how this sadness of ours over the eclipse of beauty may rise to literally maddening sorrow in this man, whose pre-eminence in art and literature has been chiefly gained by his expression of that passion for the external aspects of nature, which is one of the most marked movements of our age.

Whether in rhythmic language like our splendid

succession of naturalistic poets, or in colour like the landscape painters, the fundamental idea is the same, and not in art only but in science—it is not by hazard that Darwin is countryman and contemporary of Wordsworth and Turner, and Lyell of Scott, their differences in product are determined by details of character or circumstances of youth—all naturalism is akin.

Yet this is more than an age of naturalism, a change is in progress upon this at first almost exclusively dominant purpose. The pre-Raphaelites commence indeed with exquisite delineation of fern and pool, but one soon passes into sacred art, or the next into modern portraiture; and in the life and works of the poets we find the same transformation. For Scott the historic drama, for Wordsworth the problems of individual life, for Byron or Victor Hugo political aspirations more and more supersede the enthusiasm for nature with which all alike commenced in youth. The scientists have done absolutely the same. Darwin's " Naturalist's Voyage " in youth, his " Origin of Species " in middle life, and his " Descent of Man " in later years, mark the stages of a similar evolution in which his lesser contemporaries, Lyell and Virchow, Huxley and Hæckel, all alike fully share. This, too, explains the passage from natural science to economics, which is the main idea of the present essay; it is identical too with the passage from biology to sociology, proclaimed and investigated by Comte or Spencer; in all cases minds opened and disciplined by contact with this or that aspect of nature are betaking themselves to some kindred aspect of the supreme study of man. And thus the two economic reformers we have been discussing, Mr. Ingram and Mr. Ruskin, widely different though they may at first seem to us and to each other, are both closely akin. Both may well be unintelligible and useless to minds like those of the orthodox economist, the average journalist, and the "practical man," a trio wont to suppose themselves in permanent possession of the science. These latter are, as we have seen, provided with metaphysical conceptions of nature, of man, and of society, inherited from the Revolutionary and earlier periods, and "modern" by mere misadventure; the two former (the one consciously, the other perhaps in many respects unconsciously) having rid themselves of these, and possessed themselves of some scientific ones, are in a state to attempt genuine construction.

In our search for ideas, which will serve towards the construction of scientific economics, we have to ask, and with greater scepticism, what ideas can Mr. Ruskin offer? Destructive criticisms are not enough; can this man of art and letters really have any science, any genuine knowledge of fact and nature whereon to build? However much the quiet evangelical London home, and the antique university where our author spent his early years, may have prepared him for work in literature and art, it is evident that they did not furnish much training in science; it is indeed not unlikely that poor Thomas Edward in Banff, with many shoes indeed to make and mend, but with a museum to keep and fill, is, so far as pure science is concerned, no more of "a self-made man" than our author; for even now one sometimes feels tempted to say to an Oxford graduate of much newer brand: "Thou wast altogether born in sin, and dost thou teach us?" Yet evidencing some mathematical discipline, we have a text-book of perspective; in geology some research, and in mineralogy the only English attempt at its popularisation; in botany and zoology several books, disappointing indeed, yet with exquisite figures and flashes of observation, keen, loving, and reflective as that of the naturalist of Selborne. As concerns the needful preliminary science, then, our author, considering drawbacks, has done wonders; so much grasp of facts and of their order in nature, such consummate power of observation and description, together with wide knowledge of literature and language, history and art, constitute more preparation alike in preliminary and social sciences than most of us can show. Often, indeed, in some perplexing mixture of commentary with text, the complex sentences come thick and fast like snow-flakes, broken and soiled by the storm-beaten and soot-stained atmosphere where they have had to form, too often only to melt and disappear in turbid rivulets amid the labyrinthine crevices of mind, yet still we need no lens of loving critic, but only open eyes, to find many a thought, clear and perfect as an ice-crystal.

But to our long-delayed construction. Logic we shall not chop, and definitions we shall not concoct at starting; of mathematics even we need little, for statistics is only a highly-developed counting of fingers, and the "laws of supply and demand," derived as they must be from the observed fact that m units of the commodity A are, at given place and time, exchanging for n units of the commodity B, are expressed only by the scanty changes which can be rung on the very simple equation $m A = n B$. These well diluted, the orthodox economist is wont to skip across to what does duty with him for psychology; to the hypothetical, self-interested, purely egoistic, economic "man," and his simple wants and desires—all of "wealth"; prefacing this with copious explanations that "there is no such thing as intrinsic value," that "value does not reside in commodities themselves, and is no more to be found in a loaf of bread than in a diamond, in water, or in air," and so on. Mr. Ruskin, on the other hand, claims it as the highest merit of his leading treatise that it "gives at the outset, and maintains as the foundation of all subsequent reasoning, a definition of Intrinsic Value and intrinsic Contrary-of-Value."

How are we to reconcile this discrepancy? As in the world-old dispute of the gold and silver shield both interpretations are partially true. To say that no value exists in loaf or diamond by itself is to state for particular phenomena the idealistic aspect of phenomena in general; it is a mere commonplace of idealism which neither Mr. Ruskin nor anybody else can dispute. But the economist, continuing to explain that things have no other value, *i.e.*, that phenomena have no other aspect, merely expresses the indisputable fact that they have no other aspect for him; that the question of what loaf and diamond may mean to physicist and physiologist has not occurred to him: these studies, being alike extra-academic and extra-commercial, have indeed "not come within his province;" and assuredly, without much preparation, "he cannot hope to become a specialist." Let us however leave the inmates of the academic cloister; walk out into the world, look about us, try to express loaf and diamond from the objective side in terms of actual fact, and we find that physical and physiological properties or "values" can indeed indefinitely be assigned : the one is so much fuel, its heat-giving power measurable in calorimeter, or in actual units of work, the other a definite sensory stimulus, varying according to Fechner's law. [*dumond* written as marginal note] This is precisely what our author means in such a passage as the following, which however absurd to the orthodox, is now intelligible enough to us:—

"Intrinsic value is the absolute power of anything to support life. A sheaf of wheat of given quality and weight has in it a measurable power of sustaining the substance of the body; a cubic foot of pure air, a fixed power of sustaining its warmth; and a cluster of flowers of given beauty, a fixed power of enlivening or animating the senses and heart."

It is among the chief claims to honourable memory of the late Mr. Stanley Jevons, whose intellectual stature, head and shoulders above most of his contemporaries and survivors, gave him many a glimpse of fact denied to them, that he called attention to the wasting coal supplies of Britain, and demanded their economization, thus gripping the essential fact that our coal is not merely an object of subjective value and therefore exchange, but the fixture and embodiment of a definite quantity of stored energy, within which our modern industrial activities find a stern and calculable limit. The question of coal economy is then not in any wise the maximising of the wealth of individual coal masters and coal percentagers as Mr. Ricardo would have explained; neither the increasing of miners' wages, as their official economists (not so common certainly in this country) would say; but in the relation of actual supply to existing and future demand: in detailed criticism of the nature and purposes of such demand, and the taking definite action against that waste (of ninety-nine per cent. or so) in diffused heat, and still better diffused soot, amid which the economist of market-place and academe complacently preaches "*laissez-faire*," and Mr. Ruskin the reverse.

Again, since the activities of a community are the sum of the separate activities of its units, and since production exists for and is determined by consumption, political economy is from the present physical point of view, the generalised aspect of domestic economy, a proposition which Mr. Ruskin, following the Greek economists, has traced into valuable detail, but which ordinary writers are wont comparatively to ignore.

But let us work out our physical economics more closely. From the point of view of matter and energy our society is a vast clock being wound up and running down; the mechanical equivalent of heat holds everywhere; between machines and the automata who mind them there is no physical difference. The ideal of practice must be expressed not in terms of the process or the automata which take part in it, but in that of the result; evidently then it is of maximum production per unit time. Thus machines, men, women and children alike are to be worked to the full: "Wages are what maintain the labourer," says Mr. Ricardo, for once no metaphysician, but a physicist—since they are all mechanisms alike, no fuel is to be wasted upon them. To maximise production we need simply "Bastilles for Labour built by Capital," and of course freedom of contract, so that the worker may be free to contract between work there and starvation anywhere else. As well interfere with a man's machinery as between him and the women and children he employs. Factory acts have no justification here, no ground but "sentiment," and so even Mr. Bright, kindly-hearted, but orthodox and logical, must stoutly oppose them. For once then the orthodox economist appears to have science on his side, but let us pass to the consideration not only of the quantity but of the quality of production. What is production for? Even from our present point of view the only possible answer is for consumption, that is for the maintenance of society. Necessities of life, say the economists, "are indefinable." But the maintenance of organisms, like machines, is really under perfectly definable physical conditions; so much fuel or food, *i.e.*, such and such proteids, amyloids, fats and water: so much non-conducting covering and shelter from climate, and all is done. These requirements vary only with latitude; why, then, as Mr. Mulhall's "Balance-Sheet of the World" tells us, do Russian, Norseman and Scot, living on the same latitude, consume per head per annum in round numbers to the extent of £7, £18, and £30, respectively? Since the Russian succeeds in living, he evidently gets his necessaries: the balance then of the wealth of three Russians is at the Scotsman's credit; how is this consumed? In more complex food, in finer raiment, and in costlier dwelling; not in necessities but in plus-necessities, not in the primary function of mere maintenance, but in the secondary, yet far vaster function of nervous stimulus: it is spent in giving every product around us its costly "*æsthetic sub-function.*" But the reader may object that this is not obvious in the things around us? Certainly not. He will find that even with an art-critic to help him, little enough is visible: the author, however, prides himself greatly upon the scientific acumen which has enabled him to detect it in the articles of ordinary Edinburgh consumption, such as ashlar housefronts with iron railings, furniture and "decorations," cookery and dress. Of course it is not denied that their æsthetic element is practically latent, but the requisite three-fourths of "productive" toil no less remain.

In short, then, production, while primarily for maintenance is mainly for *æsthesis*, and the vulgar cry for so-called "utility," and the orthodox contempt and popular indifference to things beautiful, alike usually mean either a demand for the gratification of the lower senses in preference to that of the higher, or a mere habitual adherence to routine consumption without any sensory gratification at all.

Even then on the most strictly physical hypothesis, though man-days are only as horse-power, the consumption of "plus-necessaries" is three times more important than that of necessaries; a penny saved is as good as a penny gained; criticism of the æsthetic consumption thus becomes the most needful of all conceivable contributions to production; and it is therefore for the economist to become an art-critic, or, failing him, the art-critic must supply his place and become an economist. Art-criticism, in short, is a special province of the practical economics of production and consumption,—belongs to it as food-analysis does.

It is true the orthodox economist says this does not come within his province, but we must remember that he cannot hope to become a specialist.

This economic character of art-criticism is however everywhere clearly appreciated by our author. Not only must a student of the Oxford School of Art learn by drawing facts from nature or facts from history, copying of South Kensington "ornament" not being allowed, but we are constantly told that the function of art is "either to state a true thing or adorn a serviceable one," and before even attempting so much we must "clean our cities, clothe the poor, organise the idle, paint and fiddle to them afterwards." This, at any rate, is not æsthetes' twaddle of "art for art's sake" but utilitarianism pure and simple; were the solid Bentham, or the stern and inartistic Carlyle, were any soldier or engineer our professor of fine art, he could not say more. And what practical suggestions? Not disuse of machinery, as the newspaper hearsay goes, but, after an emphatic reiteration of Mill's terrible dictum—that it is doubtful whether the use of machinery has yet lightened the day's toil of a single human being, we have not only proposals for the ordered use of all natural forces, but a veritable Utopia of engineering like that of Lesseps or Da Vinci—"suggestions for the use of machinery on a colossal scale for accomplishing mighty and useful works hitherto unthought of," proposals for the embankment and irrigation of Northern Italy and the like, which may or may not be practicable of course, but to which in the latter case the exact reverse of the popularly received criticism has to be applied.

But let us pass to consider what our rival economists have to offer us from the biological standpoint—what they think of the actual population. Is not Mr. Ruskin, like a born romanticist, instead of soberly speaking of the economic units as labourers and capitalists, producers and consumers, ever fain to foist mediæval notions of rank and nobleness of blood upon us; instead of recognising "the equality of all men and the equal productiveness of all non-criminal work," is he not for ever quoting Plato or Xenophon to enforce his horror of what he is pleased to call base industry, and especially of those very mechanical and metallurgical crafts whereby we have our wealth—an outspoken heresy after which loud outcry is little to be wondered at. Not only is such work vile and debasing, not only are such Britons no better than perpetual slaves, but that unexampled progress of our modern cities which we owe to these very industries and their prosecutors, only serves to bring his denunciations to a climax. Their factories, railways, or dwellings are all alike accursed; and the revolt against the nineteenth century culminates in some sardonic exhortation to the folk of Glasgow to "burn their city," or some grim desire to "destroy without rebuilding, the new town of Edinburgh, and the city of New York." To indulgent readers this seems merely hyperæsthetic fuss, to graver and more practical minds it sounds like the scream of an hysterical petroleuse: both alike will gladly turn to the orthodox economist. Of laws of population—of the "iron law of competition" he has much to tell us—and as space presses he must have full credit for it without scrutiny. But this is all. What has biology to say? This views the community not as productive automata, but as organisms which have reached ascendency after long struggle for existence, through survival of the fittest, and in virtue of peculiarly high evolution of nervous system, and of it alone. This is "man's place in nature," whether Mr. Ruskin like it or no; and his economic positions, like any others, have now to be judged by this evolutionary standard.

Our labourers first are not the flying shuttlecocks of a hypothetical abstract science, but the actual concrete *Homo* of natural and civil history: and the economic unit is no longer "Plato's" but Darwin's man. To see the result of this mode of study of worker, work, and surroundings, "organism, function, and environment," as it is technically termed, we may first briefly quote from a recent " Analysis of the Principles of Economics "* from this very biological point of view :—

"Just as the operations of heredity upon man and other organisms are not merely analogous but identical, so also are those of function. Division of labour has specialised the polymorphic castes of the ant-hill; so the same specialisation of function develops the same polymorphic changes among men. Every one is more or less conscious of this : it is never difficult to distinguish a soldier from a joiner, or a ploughman from a weaver, while the physician reaches almost incredible skill in reading the finer results of occupation on bodily structures, normal and pathological alike. . . . Without the slightest postulation of morals, it is a biological fact, that as 'function makes the organ,' it also shapes the organism, and modifies it either for evolution or for degeneration ; moreover, other things equal, it determines its quantity of health, and limits its length of life. Ploughmen and weavers, joiners or soldiers then are incipient castes, as surely as Brahmin and Pariah, queen, worker, and drone are formed ones; and the disadvantages of the division of labour, slowly forced into prominence (as, little to the credit of biologists, they have been) through the sufferings of the many, and the moral enthusiasm of the unscientific few, demand study and classification among the 'Variations of Animals and Plants under Domestication.' The influences of the ordinary environment probably exceed those of heredity or function in importance. The importance of food and of the quality of the atmosphere is becoming recognised, so also with light; the gardener blanches his celery, the zoologist stops the development of the tadpole by withdrawing light, the sphygmograph shows how the pulse bounds at every gleam of sunshine, and the physiologist and physician are not hesitating to generalise and apply these results to the development of human life in towns.

It has been assumed by past economists that the 'necessities of life' were simply food, shelter, etc., and that these subtler factors of the environment need not be included. This pre-biological ignorance need not be argued with, for the economic problem of the maintenance of men is but one special case of the vast problem of the modification of organism by environment, exactly as the descent of man is a special case of the origin of species."

* Proceedings of the Roy. Soc. Edin. 1884.

The same analysis goes on to the "mode of modification of organisms by environment" along its two main lines of evolution or degeneration, and discusses the factors of these in some detail. It suffices to note in the second place, that it is pointed out that "while no definition of production is possible from the physical point of view since it demands a knowledge of the organism to which production is adapted, now, however, it is definable as the adaptation of the environment to the functions of the organism, every productive action thus tending towards evolution or the reverse," and that practical economics thus involves a criticism of production and consumption from the present biological standpoint. Practical economics, in short, finds its supreme end and aim in the maintenance and evolution of humanity.

Production and occupation, then, are judged, not by their immediate material result to particular individuals, whether queens or drones of the social hive; but by the aggregate result in better or worse adapted environment. Again, "not only must the factors of modification of the organism be observed and discussed, but their modifiability must be discussed and acted upon; thus in the case when any given environment or function, however apparently productive, is really fraught with disastrous influence to the organism, its modification must be attempted, and, failing that, its abandonment faced."

Without going so far as to suggest that the writer of this learned analysis might almost be making his elaborate biological paper on the somewhat simple principle of translating Mr. Ruskin into his peculiar dialect of Scientific, the general correspondence in principle and detail between biological principles on the one hand, and Mr. Ruskin's most "unpractical" teaching on the other, is most remarkable. For it is to be observed if these Darwinians are indeed to draw full consequences from their greatest law—that organism is made by function and environment, then man, if he is to remain healthy and become civilised, must not only aim at the highest standard of cerebral as well as non-cerebral excellence, and so at function healthy and delightful, but must take especial heed of his environment; not only at his peril keeping the natural factors of air, water, and light at their purest, but caring only for "production of wealth" at all, in so far as it shapes the artificial factors, the material surroundings of domestic and civic life, into forms more completely serviceable for the Ascent of Man.

And since the belly and members are dominated by a brain developed and maintained through the constant and varied stimulus of the senses, the practical ideal changes wholly. Our community, where some are so empty and weary, others so idle and full, yet all alike degenerating in their dismal cities with their long unlovely streets, their darkened and fetid air, instead of merely furnishing themes for hymns of progress and occasion for *laissez-faire*, shows clear necessity for criticism more searching, and action more systematic than that of Mr. Ruskin. And, moreover, not only do factory acts and many other "sentimental interferences with competition and freedom of contract" become at once scientific and practical, but our theory of production culminates in the Rehabilitation of Beauty, and our productive action for country and city in the restoration of nature, and the organisation of art.

It is interesting then to note that the shout of "Sentiment *versus* Science," with which Mr. Ruskin has been for so many years turned out of court, did after all accurately enough describe the controversy: science and sentiment have assuredly been on opposite sides. In one respect alone the public and the orthodox defendants have been generally mistaken; the inductive logic and statistics, the physics and chemistry, the biology and medicine, the psychology and education, were all essentially on the side of Mr. Ruskin; while on the other were too often sheer blindness to the actual facts of human and social life—organism, function and environment alike—concealed by illusory abstractions, baseless assumptions, and feeble metaphors stuck together with scholastic logic ("science" only in the metaphysician's sense, well nigh as technical as the pugilist's), and frozen into dismal and repellent form by a theory of moral sentiments which assumed moral temperature at its absolute zero.

But our economist was very much excited, was he, good practical friends? You still think he was incoherent, hyperæsthetic, and even hysterical, that he seemed only to rave and curse? That indeed was a pity; our new generation of economists and physiologists, hygienists and physicians, art-workmen, architects, and engineers are tame and quiet enough, as a generation bred in such subduing environment of light, atmosphere, and civic magnificence, must needs be; and none of that unbecoming energy of out-door exposition in which prophets of the old dispensation were apt to indulge, is to be expected from them,—yet assuredly teaching and practice essentially the same, towards ideals wholly identical.

For the present state of production is by no means good enough. A modern city, however stupendous its wealth—on paper—has after all hardly any ultimate products to show save a sorry aggregate of ill-constructed houses, mean without, and unhealthy within, and containing but little of permanent value; for the rest, hideous dirt and darkness, smoke and sewage everywhere, as if its inhabitants had absolutely framed an ideal of a short life and a dismal one, with which they are dull enough to rest contented. Men are everywhere awaking to see that this is no longer to be endured, and it is the central merit of our author to have at once inaugurated that criticism of production, and that practical action for its improvement which has been setting in so hopefully of recent years. The so-called "æsthetic revival," with its outcomes like the Kyrle and other "Environment Societies," represent in fact the small beginnings of the Industrial Reformation, of that re-organisation of production—of products and processes, of environment and function, which is the nearest task of the united art and science of the immediate future.

Again, a demand for commodities is a command of labour; it determines function, and therefore quality of organism. Hence Mr. Ruskin's continued insistence upon the primary duty of regulating expenditure with studied reference to its effect upon the mind and body of the labourer, so at once seeking the minimum service from the lower occupations, and maximising that from the higher ones; and his criticism of "the kinds of work which are severally best accomplished by hand or by machine; together with the effect of machinery in gathering and multiplying population and its effect upon the minds and bodies of such population." Such teaching equals or exceeds at once in clear biological insight and in social wisdom anything else in the entire literature of practical economics; since it clearly indicates the line of evolution towards the future city of healthy and happy artists, surrounded by imperishable treasure, from our modern city of weary and sickly drudges, immersed in dirt for their pains.

It would be easy to go on gathering such scientific and practical suggestions, to show, for instance, how "pieces of sentimental nonsense" about "purity of race," or that about "bachelors and rosières" in "Time and Tide," at once analyse the conditions and attack the problem of the evolution of society by heredity and sexual selection. But any reader can follow these out for himself, see how the "sentimental political economy" contained at once the germs of systematic science and of its noblest applications, and find more and more as he reads that our despised and rejected author, however noteworthy and memorable for theoretic work in art, is yet more so for his practical applications of the knowledge to the art of life; that our disciple of Plato and scholar of Turner has also become the highest practical exponent of Darwin.

But the St. George's Company? The writer has no personal knowledge of them (save that they do at least succeed in making sterling cloth, which not only bears scrutiny by experts, but—archaic spinning-wheel and loom notwithstanding—is among the cheapest in the market); but so far as he can make out, their main ideas may be simply stated thus,—seeing, they say, that some occupations are pleasanter and healthier than others, and notably agricultural rather than mechanical ones, we intend having these; you, if you will, "fill your lungs with cotton-fur, your hearts with rage and mutiny, become gnomes of Europe, slaves of the lamp!" We mean to have the best environment that is going, and the healthiest functions we can find; and not sacrificing ourselves to production, but subordinating it to us, we shall produce an increasing store of real wealth, of permanent ultimate products. Finally, paying much attention to the quality of the organism, its good breeding and education, we and our children shall accordingly survive in the struggle for existence, while you mechanical townsfolk and your economists become extinct. Hence, as the latter are nothing if not "practical," the St. George's Guild must be hopelessly "unpractical," in the technical sense in which we have uniformly been finding the terms employed.

But the Sheffield museum: who ever heard of such a place? At the top of a hill, and almost in the country—so that with such trouble, pulse must quicken and breath freshen and brain awaken before one sees the strange new sights—how much better the spacious, easily accessible galleries of Kensington, how much more inviting, how much more suitable—for loafers! And, after all, only a few objects to compare with the multifarious wealth of the endless cases of a great museum. Merely the teaching by a series of carefully selected types—exactly parallel to the small and compact selections which are now replacing for teaching purposes, the vast museums (henceforth storehouses for reference) in every modern scientific school. No wonder, again, some "common-sense" people cannot cease to deplore the old-fashioned impracticability of Mr. Ruskin!

But let us pass to education. What is to be said of a teacher who speaks lightly of the three R's, and who threatens to make even the first of them optional? Here surely is reaction to ignorance with a vengeance.

Let the reader make what deduction he pleases for personal idiosyncracy, for passion and paradox; but let him also take some note of existing facts, and consider whether he would not do well also to place his protest —if forceful and stormy, perhaps all the better—against the miserable mixture of pseudo-literary and pseudo-commercial cram, "classical" and "modern" by courtesy or irony, miscalled "education:" that jumbled compromise into which academic fossil and commercial Philistine everywhere settle down for the supposed maintenance of their supposed interests, and the actual stupefaction of their children's lives. But what would he give us instead? Of this twice clerkly lore there would perhaps not be enough? The craft of parsing would indeed be in danger; the names of French departments and the tables of obsolete weights and measures might come less pat upon the tongue; yet for all we should be immeasurably nearer in method and result to that noble discipline of complete soul in perfected body, which the wise men of all ages have had for their highest ideal, calling it Education.

For two distinct tendencies are at work in our modern universities and schools, the dominant one deliberately preferring memory of mere words for observation of facts and reasoning therefrom, which should be supplied by *discipline* in science, and more memory of words for that co-ordination of hand and eye which is supplied by practice in the arts, and substituting verbal test of competitive examination for practical test in life. One is the school of Cram, evolving towards a Chinese, the other the school of Culture, evolving towards a Greek ideal; or more accurately towards Tartarean and Olympian ideals respectively. Between the representatives of the former, portly word-fog-giants, bearing the awful names of Professor, Head-master, Inspector, and what not, swinging the mighty mace of authority, crusted in triple mail of hood and gown, and bearing many a magic amulet of diplomas, and the scattered knight-errants like Comte or Spencer, like Pestalozzi or like Ruskin, who now and then attack them, the battle must indeed be long : yet when each colossus of intellectual fat has fallen before the strokes of intellectual muscle, when our orthodox educationists have gone the way of the orthodox economists, and when schools at once really classical and modern have arisen to give that genuine knowledge of nature and of literature which make alike scientist and scholar, that genuine discipline in arts coarse and fine which makes the worker, and that factual grip of history and society which makes the citizen, we shall after all only be having in more systematic form the essential curriculum of a St. George's School.

Leaving the reader to continue such defensive criticisms, it is time for us briefly to summarise. We have found that while on one hand the stronghold of orthodox political economy turns out to be little better than an air-castle of mediæval metaphysics, collapsing at the slightest breath of scientific criticism, on the other Mr. Ruskin furnishes much solid material for the new construction. Little attempt can however yet be made at assigning his place in economic literature and history. His destructive criticisms have undoubtedly been of considerable service to many readers in this country, but it must be remembered that these were mainly necessary because of the popular ignorance of Germany. There the defects of the Manchester school had long ago been exposed by the historical and the socialistic schools ; while in France its lingering survivors have lately been receiving the *coup de grace* from M. de Laveleye; and the criticisms of Cliffe Leslie, Ingram, and even Jevons, have been in this country producing the same result. His chief services then are constructive. Exceeding all other economists in clear vision of physical realities, in insight and criticism of the quality of production and of life, he is more than any other writer the legitimate continuator of the Physiocratic school, and the forerunner of its complete re-systematisation by the aid of physical and biological science; while his statement of the aims of practical economics in terms of quality of life, his treatment of criticism of art and other aspects of production from the same point of view, and his clear enunciation of the essential unity of economics and morals in opposition to the discord assumed as a deductive artifice, will remain especially and permanently classic.

His filiation to Carlyle and others might have been traced, while some of the results of his teaching, not only in modern art-criticism, and consequently improved production, but upon more strictly economic studies and practical effort might have been outlined. Yet even if space allowed, this would be premature; for his influence cannot be measured until the younger generation whom he has educated to active social sympathy, has brought forth its manifold results of economic research and practical application. Everywhere, too, organic filaments are spinning; reform in the production of wealth, and economy in its consumption are alike in progress; more slowly indeed, yet surely, views of its distribution at once more rational and more generous are gaining ground: the health and culture of the worker, the ennoblement of function, the purification of environment have at last won clear recognition as truly practical. Nor is the corresponding effort far off.

For as once men's hearts burned within them as they went forth under antique priestly guidance to win back the Holy City, and again in dim philosophic light at the Revolution to win their freedom, so once again throughout Europe a new enthusiasm is arising, deeper and wider than of old. Though foreseen with varying clearness, and sought with yet more varying success, the ideal has ever been fundamentally the same; the kingdom of God upon earth, the achievement of fraternity, the evolution of humanity are but the changing names for the unending struggle after that union of the material and the moral order which is the task and problem of life. In our day, both task and problem are far vaster than of old; and though a corresponding wealth of material resource has been in our hands, there has been little light to guide its application, and that mainly from dying lamps. The coming time is more hopeful; the sorely needed knowledge, both of the natural and the social order, is approaching maturity; the long-delayed renaissance of art has begun, and the prolonged discord of these is changing into harmony. So with these for guidance, men shall no more grind on in slavery to a false image of their lowest selves, miscalled Self-interest, but at length, as freemen, live in the Sympathy and labour in the Synergy of the Race.

And for this, the last Crusade, herald, knight, and preacher are not wanting; yet in our land and day there has been no clearer herald, nobler preacher, or truer knight than John Ruskin, Economist.

PATRICK GEDDES.

"Give to barrows, trays, and pans
    Grace and glimmer of romance;
    Bring the moonlight into noon
Hid in gleaming piles of stone;
On the city's pavèd street
Plant gardens lined with lilacs sweet;
Let spouting fountains cool the air,
Singing in the sun-baked square;
Let statue, picture, park, and hall,
Ballad, flag, and festival,
The past restore, the day adorn,
And make to-morrow a new morn.
So shall the drudge in dusty frock
Spy behind the city clock
Retinues of airy kings,
Skirts of angels, starry wings,
His fathers shining in bright fables,
His children fed at heavenly tables.
'Tis the privilege of Art
Thus to play its cheerful part,
Man on earth to acclimate,
And bend the exile to his fate,
And moulded of one element
With the days and firmament,
Teach him on these as stairs to climb,
And live on even terms with Time;
Whilst upper life the slender rill
Of human sense doth overfill."

EMERSON.

IV.

WALT WHITMAN

POET AND DEMOCRAT

STRONG poet of the sleepless gods that dwell
    As far above the stars as we beneath,
    Thy melody, disdaining the soft sheath
Of dainty modern music, snaps the spell,
And heedless of old forms and fettered plan,
    Clothes itself carelessly in rough free words,
    And strikes with giant's hand the inner chords
That vibrate in the strong and healthful man !

What if our brothers in an age to be,
    Emerging from the Titan war of Thought,
        Seize hollow Custom, and with one keen blow
    Strike off her seven heads, and having smote,
        Pass on, and with their larger veins aglow
With new-found vigour, mould themselves to thee !

A. A.

*H*AVE *we not hailed them great who fought for the truth
  when it was not,*
 Strong in the rapture of hope, knowing by faith it should be,
Barriers down, ways clear; and shall we not hail you, brother,
 True to the high faith of freedom, 'midst of the shame of the free—
*After the truth's own treason, hoping against hope's confusion, teaching
 the weary of light and the hope-sick to see.*

Laurels we gave them freely, who, when their kindred reviled them,
 Fronted the scorn of the world with a scorn overwhelming its own:
Shall we not laurel the leader, who, when his brothers denied him,
 Loving them never the less, stayed him not ev'n to condone;
*Glad of their virtue still, triumphing not in their vileness, triumphing
 only to think they should walk in the way he had shown!*

Better forgiveness serene as the sun than the bolt of the storm-god:
 Better the large faith of love than the Coriolanian cry:
Better the eye still bright with the dream of a glorious distance
 Than the sad grey world of the sage scanning his race from on high;
*Better the pride of the comrade, great in his vision of greatness, than the
 pride of the sage or the scorner, letting his kind pass by.*

WALT WHITMAN.

AN ancient and authoritative saw has formulated for us a peculiar social tendency which, though presumably recognised for eighteen hundred years back, has not, even in this era of explanation and theory, been systematically accounted for. It is exemplified in the common disposition to-day in England to see the greatest living American author in one whom the literary world of the States continues to treat somewhat as an outer barbarian. American writers have not yet ceased to speak with a half-indignant, half-scornful astonishment of the singular appreciation British readers and critics accord to products of American literature which are thought little of in the land of their birth. And yet the law of the ratio of a prophet's popularity has been illustrated parallel-wise in the States, the reading public there frequently taking a British writer into favour long before he has won acceptance at home. Reversing the phrase of Hamlet, one might suggest that there is something natural in this, if philosophy could but find it out. That Carlyle should have found a wide hearing in America earlier than in England, might perhaps be explained plausibly by crediting the people of the young Republic with the more ready ear for unconventional speech; but how on that theory account for the tabooing of Whitman in the States in the teeth of the tribute of that Emerson who had stood sponsor for Carlyle? Perhaps 'twere to consider too curiously for literary edification to consider so. To know why Whitman has been so much more kindly received in England than in the States would probably be to have a true perception of his value and importance, his strength and his weakness; but to attain such an explanation seems much more difficult than to weigh his message and his method on their merits. To know why we have ourselves received him, however, is a step towards a solution; and it is meet that so much should be ascertained.

It is a natural as well as a precedented course to begin by asking what we went out to see when we met the stranger; but how shall it be told? At the outset we are met by the sharp American demand to know why we should expect a peculiar literary product from a section of our own race which speaks our speech, and reads our classics, in a climate not greatly different from our own. The position is delicate. Are we to premise that our kin beyond seas are further-seeing than we; or to hint the crude doctrine that we look for large ideas from the dwellers in a large land, novel thoughts from those who breathe the air of the New World? Crude or clumsy if the process of reasoning be, there the fact stands that English readers had long been demanding from the United States a new and autochthonic poetical product; and it can hardly be but that the demand arose from a sense of distinction and high birthright attaching to the young nation whose gianthood was so early surmised. Surely the attitude of expectation had its touching side, though we may not find it stand rational question. The instinctive faith in the boundless possibilities opened up by this new avatar of democracy is in unison with the spirit of Whitman's own poetry; and it was so far natural— though our first perplexity remains—that those who looked wistfully or curiously across the Atlantic for a new song, should have affinities for the American man who came forward to proclaim that new songs must be sung, and essayed to begin.

Still, we are a perverse generation. No less loud than our demand for an American poetry have been our protests against Americanism in speech and manners; and when there appears in America a poet who is obtrusively, and must for certain be genuinely, American, were it only because he is clearly nothing else, we greet him with an urbanity and an enthusiasm that he cannot evoke in his own habitat. Even were there no incredulous Americans to challenge us we might well ask ourselves whether our attachment has not been too unadvised, too sudden.

It may reasonably be conceded, at the outset, that there is a tolerably strong presumption against the man who in these days comes forward both to prescribe the task of modern poetry and to do it. True, there has arisen a demand such as was never formulated before, that the age shall produce its special poet; and it would seem necessary that he who shall sing the age should know what he is about; as the poet of Paradise is presumed to have had his "great argument" present to his consciousness from the first. But the doctrine that ages have their poets is only one outcome of a spirit of criticism peculiar to this century, and the same spirit is somewhat positive about the essence of poetry being spontaneity. Lord Tennyson has told us that he "does but sing because he must;" Mr. Browning has indicated a similar conception; and the general critical attitude towards Wordsworth does not promise good fortune to the man whose poetry is the systematic expression of a literary theory. Mr. Arnold has given us his prefaces, but we feel them to be critical after-thoughts. Milton had his idea of what were the essential qualities of poetry, but his choice of an epic theme was almost accidental; Wordsworth alone had a theory of his work which involved an estimate of the themes and methods of his contemporaries, and a defined principle in the choice of his own; and Wordsworth seems to have been least successful just where he was most circumspect, most distinctly conscious of fulfilling his mission. The hostile presumption is obtrusive. When before did a great poet say to himself, "My age wants a special kind of poetry. Nobody else is producing it, and I must"? Is not the very conception suggestive of the doomed prosaist who labours to turn an idea into rhyme, instead of finding, poet-wise, his thought run to song;—of Ben Jonson writing his tirades in prose and then blank-versifying them?

And yet, on after-thought it will be found that nothing more decisively identifies Whitman with his age and its literature than this backbone of critical and didactic purpose in his work. It is our century that has condemned the novel with a purpose; but it was only the other day a practised craftswoman declared with general acceptance that, however that might be, the novel without a purpose was something worse—a sufficiently compendious form of the argument that what is wanted is really the skill to effect the purpose in the reader's despite, instead of simply dunning him with a bald appeal. The most esteemed and the most notorious work of the day are alike the outcome of a self-conscious and systematised philosophy; George Eliot and M. Zola alike have "un but;" even Mr. Browning is not content to be regarded as psychologising for psychology's sake; and if the mind which wanted to know what was proved by Paradise Lost might with equal propriety put its question with regard to the poetry of this generation, at least, with its forensic turn, it could not miss seeing that the poets generally wanted to prove something. In short, we are brought up against the discovery that all poetry is criticism of life, and must be content with demanding that the criticism shall take a less formidably crude shape than an Essay on Man.

No poet is more explicit about his creed and purpose than Whitman; perhaps none has such an all-absorbing creed and purpose to proclaim; and when that is once perceived the doubt about his poetic quality is already half-disposed of. If there was a truth in Carlyle's favourite citation from Milton—that "he who would write a heroic poem must make his life a heroic poem"—it is surely still truer that he who would sing democracy must be the most robust democrat; and Whitman is the very democrat of practice as well as of faith and philosophy.

A half-ratiocinative, half-emotional attachment to the cause of free self-government is one of the commonest states of mind in these days; but after all that has been said in humanitarian literature it is doubtful whether a cordial feeling of human brotherhood has nearly come to be the normal one for the majority. As a character is made to observe in a recent novel, " A man may be a democrat without being a demophile." Our love for the general run of our fellow-creatures remains distinctly theoretical: our friendships are about as purely expressive of our private idiosyncracies, as entirely matter of individual leaning, as were those of our forefathers who believed in the divine right of kings; indeed, we tend to be much less effusive in our attachments than they, greatly toning down the language of friendship without being at all more addicted to all-round camaraderie. Our democratic poetry has mostly run to generalities. But Whitman is in nothing more remarkable than in the exaltation, the fervour, with which he sings of love between comrades. It is practically, as he sounds it, a new note in modern poetry; and were it for nothing else he might well be forgiven on the strength of his elevation of feeling in this regard, for any seeming lack of it in other connections. His faculty of brotherly love is one of his most potent inspirations. Lincoln's homely qualities live in the memory of good democrats who feel the transfiguring effect of his death; but Whitman, while never once alluding to the assassin, sings passionately of the dead president as of a beloved friend, "the wisest, sweetest soul" of his generation. His whole nature tends to rapturous expression: in very truth he cannot choose but express himself as he does. From his first line he is not only the vowed singer of democracy and the dear love of comrades, but the self-poised, self-centred, self-possessed democratic unit; a manifestation of the force which *is* democracy; the typical self-asserting individual.

His leading poem begins like the Fifth Symphony, as no song ever began before, with a salvo of self-proclamation which is at the same time, and *ex facto*, the knock of fate. "I have found the law of my poems," he announces in a late prose fragment; and indeed he points to it truly enough. The paragraph should be read as it stands, as illustrating at once his penetration and his literary manner, or lack of manner.

"AN EGOTISTICAL 'FIND.'

"'I have found the law of my own poems' was the unspoken but more-and-more decided feeling that came to me as I pass'd, hour after hour, amid all this grim, yet joyous elemental abandon—this plenitude of material, entire absence of art, untrammel'd play of primitive nature—the chasm, the gorge, the crystal mountain stream, repeated scores, hundreds of miles—the broad handling and absolute uncrampedness—the fantastic forms, bathed in transparent browns, faint reds and greys, towering sometimes a thousand, sometimes two or three thousand feet high—at their tops now and then huge masses pois'd, and mixing with the clouds, with only their outlines, hazed in misty lilac, visible. ('In nature's grandest shows,' says an old Dutch writer, an ecclesiastic, 'amid the ocean's depth, if so might be, or countless worlds rolling above at night, a man thinks of them, weighs all, not for themselves or the abstract, but with reference to his own personality, and how they may affect or colour his destinies.')"

The major part of the explanation perhaps lies in the suffixed quotation; the minor in Whitman's own characteristically rambling and formless sentence. Whitman sings life, history, politics as he does because he is the man he is, absolutely self-confident, sanguine, candid, loving, tolerant and eupeptic; yet self-esteeming, vigorously egotistic, and exclusive by fits. All life for him relates itself to his impulses; his is the naïf popular theism of the day which finds the universe made for man, and the land for the race. Again, he has, as he points out, that very sameness in caprice which marks primitively self-assertive and genuine natures, as that of Carlyle, of whom Emerson remarked that he said the same thing day after day, week after week, and year after year. And like the half-cultured continent he is profuse, straggling, miscellaneous. In another passage he has expressed his sense of the significance of his books more explicitly. Probably, he says, "the whole of these varied songs, and all of my writings, both volumes, only ring changes in some sort, on the ejaculation, How vast, how eligible, how joyful, how real is a Human Being, himself or herself."

Just, however, as he is the most actual democrat, in his independence and his brotherliness, so is Whitman the most expert scholar of democracy. Let any one who has gone through his prose say whether any writer has looked more piercingly and patiently into all the aspects of the subject, fair and foul; accumulated more facts and ideas; or placed any in a greater variety of lights. In this department—philosophy apart—no man can teach him anything. Optimism is the *raison d'être* of his work as a whole, and the ground tone of his personality, but he has been in the deeps, and at least felt pessimistic pangs in ebb-tide moods. Only after having seen all round his theme, only after having thought over it in all weathers and all companies, in sunlight and moonlight, in ecstasy and in despondency, in complacent ease, and in grey and dreary hours of sorrow, could he have reached his matchless certitude of belief. It is difficult to overrate the strength of conviction and confidence of power and knowledge a man must have to come forward as did Whitman, and sound his "Let there be light" across what he regards as a world-wide chaos of thoughts effete and transitory. According to his own account he, the strolling compositor and journalist, found the entire literature of his country (he seems even to have included Emerson, on which head more anon) their little inventions, vote for their candidate, and choose their churches and their clothes? It is, of course, sheer extravagance from any calmly critical standpoint to sum up American writers in such terms as those above quoted. Any one but the seer of democracy in a prophetic frenzy will gratefully acknowledge as contributions to the choice literature of the world the deep and delicate studies of Hawthorne, the singular products of the abnormal intellect of Poe, and the bright, bold inspiration and catholic enthusiasm of Emerson—surely a worthy son of democracy—not to mention the popular singers who have surely fulfilled one of Whitman's own tests, and helped many a human soul. Hawthorne, Poe, Emerson, and Longfellow, each worked out his mission, as Whitman desires every man should do; and even Poe, be it noted, protested against the acceptance given to anti-democratic European literature in America. But the prophet of democracy, being what he is, must needs be didactically inconsistent in order to be consistently prophetic. For Whitman to justify his intolerance of the natural bias of his literary countrymen, would probably be to land himself in the toils of fatalist metaphysics, and his admirers can scarcely hope to fare better. But the practical explanation is pretty clear. Either Whitman, being a pioneer and something of an arrogant believer in himself, has really not had the leisure or the care to study properly the literature of his own country, or, being the bearer and devoted prophet of the great ideas of democracy, he lacks the faculty to appreciate the product of those who, working like himself in the literary guild, occupy themselves discursively, and leave the great ideas more or less to shift for themselves. Or be it that the alternatives are correlative views of

Whitman's function and personality—in any case the conclusion will be found to lend itself to an estimate of his work from the literary standpoint.

Venturing on a domain of metaphor always to be trodden with circumspection, let us say that when the Zeitgeist wants to strike an important blow he makes a heavy hammer. It might seem that the self-consciousness which, involving an incapacity for what is ordinarily considered natural development, is half the time contemplating itself and missing the expansion it worships—that this is an abortive growth. But just such an absorption in one idea appears to be the necessary condition of the poet of democracy—just such a fanaticism seems needed to smite the people into that thrill of intelligent belief in their own high destiny which will make them progress towards it. The leader who would stimulate all can share the relaxations of none: he is fain to resent that those who seem capable of stimulating should not be doing so with him; just as, on the other hand, the disciplined thinker who believes in democracy and progress would fain that the poet had arrived at a fuller system of thought—that Whitman had been Comte. The one thing quite clear about the poetic function is that the poet must sing a passion, his own or another's, and the deeper the passion sung—relatively to the reader's sympathy—the more potent the poetry. Whitman's passion, then, is democracy, and it is none the less a passion because it is a formulated creed. Poetry must needs acquire the self-conscious quality which more and more colours all thought as evolution goes on; progress in life—upward progress—being but progress in consciousness. Poetry can no longer be an idea which does not know where it came from, and ends with its expression.

The essential thing is that the singer of democracy shall be full charged with his theme; and that an idea which feeds on optimism and confidence shall be carried with a confidence that no adversity will dash. And how Whitman's confidence rays out from his first page! Other poets have sung democracy in moments of expansion, or when goaded by the sight of war and depression: he alone ecstatically points a prosperous demos to new heights of ideal life.

"A live nation," he proclaims in his first preface, "can always cut a deep mark, and can have the best authority the cheapest, namely from its own soul. This is the sum of the profitable uses of individuals or states, and of present action and grandeur, and of the subjects of poets. As if it were necessary to trot back generation after generation to the eastern records! As if the beauty and sacredness of the demonstrable must fall behind that of the mythical! As if men do not make their mark out of any times! As if the opening of the western continent by discovery, and what has transpired since in North and South America, were less than the small theatre of the antique or the aimless sleep-walking of the middle ages!"

He is just as confident in his poetic mission as in his message. "Of all nations," he declares, "the United States, with veins full of poetical stuff, most need poets, and will doubtless have the greatest and use them the greatest. Their presidents shall not be their common referee so much as their poets shall. Of all mankind the great poet is the equable man. Not in him but off from him things are grotesque or eccentric, or fail of their sanity. . . . He is the arbiter of the diverse, and he is the key. He supplies what wants supplying, and checks what wants checking. It peace is the routine, out of him speaks the spirit of peace. . . . In war he is the most deadly force of the war. . . . High up out of reach he stands, turning a concentrated light. . . . The time straying towards infidelity and confections and persiflage he withholds by his steady faith. . . . His brain is the ultimate brain. He is no arguer; he is judgment. He judges not as the judge judges, but as the sun falling round a helpless thing. As he sees the farthest he has the most faith."

Some of the sentences in this latter passage, brilliantly enforced though they are by the others, are almost enough to prove, what full knowledge of his books absolutely establishes, that Whitman has almost no humour. The circumstance is peculiarly noteworthy. It is universally agreed that humour consists in the perception of the incongruous; and it has seemed natural that among the most restless population in the world, they possessing the most complex civilisation, the perception should be most highly educated. But Whitman is too enormously in earnest, too intensely faithful, to laugh. Carlyle, let it be noted, is the one really earnest moralist who has indulged much in humour, and Carlyle's humour grew out of his profound unfaith in humanity. Whitman's faith is as strong as Carlyle's scepticism; and though he may meet one of Carlyle's favourite moral tests by a capacity to laugh broadly at the broadly and simply laughable, he is never heartily humorous in his writing. The humorous propensities of his countrymen get little recognition from him; when he is in a minatory mood —he frequently is in his later prose—he sees in the American habit of jesting on all things one of the unhealthy aspects of things democratic. That this is no accidental trait in Whitman is suggested by observation of its appearance in the later utterances of George Eliot, who had in her time smiled—lovingly enough no doubt—over most of the odd aspects of humanity, but who at length shrank from the aggressive tendencies developed by the humorous spirit. Whether the truth lies in that view or in Mr. Traill's subtly presented suggestion* that humour is the true antidote to the contents of Pandora's box, is a question of somewhat deep import, which will be found involved in our inquiry at another point. It may be doubted, however, whether Whitman's lack of humour is not a weakness in him as a propagandist, relatively to the average intellect of his time. Which of us can remain resolutely grave over the intimation that, among other things, the "picturesque looseness of carriage" of the American common people, and "the president's taking off his hat to them, not they to him," are "unrhymed poetry"? The thing is said in all good faith, and a momentary sympathy is possible, though it is not clear why the president should take off his hat to his fellow-citizens save to win their votes; but the smile will break through.

Mr. Meredith makes a character observe that cynicism is intellectual dandyism. Perhaps the dictum is truer than its acute author really believed. Take it that cynicism is humour overdone, and we arrive at a conception of humour as the soul's clothing for its nakedness, acutely experienced after modern indulgence in the fruit of the tree of knowlege of good and evil. It may be that the adoption of this is demonstrably an irrational act; but to demonstrate that a joke is an absurdity is but to make the joker a present of another. Logical progress, however, is possible on the understanding that he is a weak creature, and that a stronger

* *Fortnightly Review*, September, 1882.

may get on in vigorous nakedness. Such a son of Adam is Whitman. He positively does not need humour to protect him from his atmosphere, and he has no self-critical qualms about his appearance; being, indeed, by his enemies' account, far too naked to be shamed. See what an unflinching look he has taken at the seamy side of the life of the Republic.

"Once, before the war (Alas! I dare not say how many times the mood has come!) I, too, was filled with doubt and gloom. A foreigner, an acute and good man, had impressively said to me, that day—putting in form, indeed, my own observations: 'I have travelled much in the United States, and watched their politicians, and listened to the speeches of the candidates, and read the journals, and gone into the public-houses, and heard the unguarded talk of men. And I have found your vaunted America honey-combed from top to toe with infidelism, even to itself and its own programme. I have marked the brazen hell-faces of secession and slavery gazing defiantly from all the windows and doorways. I have everywhere found, primarily, thieves and scalliwags arranging the nominations to offices, and sometimes filling the offices themselves. I have found the North just as full of bad stuff as the South. Of the holders of public office in the nation, or in the States, or their municipalities, I have found that not one in a hundred has been chosen by any spontaneous selection of the outsiders, the people, but all have been nominated and put through by little or large caucuses of the politicians, and have got in by corrupt rings and electioneering, not capacity or desert. I have noticed how the millions of sturdy farmers and mechanics are thus the helpless supple-jacks of comparatively few politicians. And I have noticed more and more the alarming spectacle of parties usurping the government, and openly and shamelessly wielding it for party purposes. Sad, serious, deep truths."—*Democratic Vistas.*

In a paper on "Origins of Attempted Secession," he presents what, without any thought of being piquant, he calls "a schedule or list" of one of the controlling "Democratic" nominating conventions of the Republic, as they existed "for a long time before, and inclusive of that which nominated Buchanan;" a catalogue and picture which, with all its mordant emphasis, carries a certain ludicrous suggestion of Falstaff's regiment, but which yet haunts the memory like a description from the *Inferno*. And in that paper he deliberately avows a belief which might surprise even those Englishmen who sided with the South, the conviction, namely—and it was formed with a wide and close knowledge of the States—"that if at the opening of the contest the abstract duality-question of slavery and quiet could have been submitted to a direct popular vote, as against their opposite, they would have triumphantly carried the day in a majority of the Northern States—in the large cities, leading off with New York and Philadelphia, by tremendous majorities. The events of '61 amazed everybody North and South, and burst all prophecies and calculations like bubbles. But even then, and during the whole war, the stern fact remains that (not only did the North put it down, but) *the secession cause had numerically just as many sympathisers in the free as in the rebel States.*"

He can even be somewhat atrabiliar in his comments on what he sees about him—and then, as it happens, he professes a disposition to laugh.

"There is, to the humorous observer of American attempts at fashion, according to the models of foreign courts and saloons, quite a comic side—particularly visible at Washington city—a sort of high life below stairs business. As if any farce could be funnier, for instance, than the scenes of the crowds, winter nights, meandering around our presidents and their wives, cabinet officers, western or other senators, representatives, etc.; born of good labouring mechanic, or farmer stock and antecedents, attempting those full-dress receptions, finesse of parlors, foreign ceremonies, etiquettes, etc."

This comes in a note on "Society," after a passage

on "Boston, with its circles of social mummies, swathed in cerements harder than brass—its bloodless religion (Unitarianism), its complacent vanity of science and literature, lots of grammatical correctness, mere knowledge (always wearisome in itself)—its zealous abstractions, ghosts of reforms."

Mr. Ruskin never said anything worse of his fellow-citizens than this:

"Confess that everywhere, in shop, street, church, theatre, barroom, official chair, are pervading flippancy and vulgarity, low cunning, infidelity—everywhere the youth puny, impudent, foppish, prematurely ripe—everywhere an abnormal libidinousness, unhealthy forms, male, female, painted, padded, dyed, chignon'd, muddy complexions, bad blood, the capacity for good motherhood deceasing or deceased, shallow notions of beauty, with a range of manners, or rather lack of manners (considering the advantages enjoyed), probably the meanest to be seen in the world." "Of these rapidly sketched portraitures, hiatuses," he says in a footnote, "the two which seem to me most serious are, for one, the condition, absence, or perhaps the singular abeyance of moral, conscientious fibre all through American Society; and, for another, the appalling depletion of women in their powers of sane athletic maternity, their crowning attribute, and ever making the woman, in loftiest spheres, superior to the man."—*Democratic Vistas.*

But with all this in mind our arch-democrat bates ultimately no jot of heart or hope. Notwithstanding it all, "the morbid facts of American politics and society everywhere are but passing incidents and flanges of our unbounded impetus of growth—weeds, annuals, of the rank rich soil—not central, enduring, perennial things." "All the hitherto experience of the States, their first century, has been but preparation, adolescence." " Enough, that while the piled embroidered shoddy gaud and fraud spreads to the superficial eye, the hidden warp and weft are genuine, and will wear for ever. Enough, in short, that the race, the land which could raise such as the late Rebellion could also put it down." "I know nothing grander, better exercise, better digestion, more positive proof of the past, the triumphant result of faith in human kind, than a well-contested American election." "During the Secession war I was with the armies, and saw the rank and file, North and South, and studied them for four years. I have never had the least doubt about the country in its essential future since."

There is no arguing down this elemental force of faith; and he must be well set on his feet who can stedfastly resist it, even with the prediction of Baron Jacobi in "Democracy" fresh in his ears. When Whitman reviews Carlyle on the latter's death, the democrat takes the superior position by sheer force of assured, tolerant serenity. No better, closer, deeper, more perspicaciously appreciative estimate of Carlyle has appeared than Whitman's in the "Specimen Days and Collect." Already he had allowed that there was value in "Shooting Niagara," in which Mr. Henry James, senior, could see but "puerile gabble;" and he now asks, "Who cares that he wrote about Dr. Francia, and 'Shooting Niagara,' and 'The Nigger Question'—and didn't at all admire our United States? I doubt if he ever thought or said half as bad words about us as we deserve." One would give something to have had Carlyle pass judgment on "Leaves of Grass," in acknowledgment of Emerson's present and criticism; but it would be still more interesting to know how he would have taken that imperturbable acceptance of his entire anti-democratic Jeremiad. To Whitman there is no sting in the fact that Carlyle and Hugo and Tennyson "cannot span the vast revolutionary arch thrown by the United States over the centuries, fixed in the present, launched to the endless future." His vast faith can swallow up their unbelief. "Fortunately the gestation of our thirty-eight empires (and plenty more to come) proceeds on its course, on scales of area and velocity immense and absolute as the globe, and, like the globe itself, quite oblivious even of great poets and thinkers. But we can by no means afford to be oblivious of them."

In his eyes all things work together for the good of democracy. The Secession war he calls the Union war. "A great literature will yet arise out of the era of those four years, those scenes—era-compressing centuries of native passion, first-class pictures, tempests of life and death—an inexhaustible mine for the histories, drama, romance, and even philosophy, of peoples to come—indeed the verteber of poetry and art (of personal character, too), for all future America—far more grand, in my opinion, to the hands capable of it, than Homer's siege of Troy, or the French wars to Shakespere." He foresees for the States a superb civilisation; he pictures the details as Christian enthusiasts do the phenomena of the New Jerusalem. "A few years, and there will be an appropriate, native, grand opera, the lusty and wide-lipp'd offspring of Italian methods. Yet it will be no mere imitation, nor follow precedents, any more than nature follows precedents. Vast oval halls will be constructed, on acoustic principles, in cities, where companies of musicians will perform lyrical pieces, born to the people of these States; and the people will make perfect music a part of their lives." "Also, a great breed of orators will one day spread over the United States, and be continued." "Also, in a few years, there will be in the cities of these States, immense museums, with suites of halls, containing samples and illustrations from all the peoples of the earth, old and new. In these halls, in the presence of these illustrations, the noblest savans will deliver lectures to thousands of young men and women on history, natural history, the sciences, etc." Such faith is scarce in Israel.

It forms a somewhat grotesque commentary on Whitman's enthusiastic accounts of the elements of greatness in American life, that the respectable, cultured, American population contrive to see in the man who talks thus nothing but a coarse propounder of loose notions on sexual morality.* Supposing there were no direct defence whatever for Whitman's offences against the convenances in "Leaves of Grass," the idea that his educated countrymen can with almost one accord make these offences outweigh his entire gospel is not easily to be grasped. A future age will assuredly see one of the sickliest of all the moral conditions of modern life in this collapse of the American nervous system before a mere defiance of one social law by the man who, of all his race, has most ardently set great ideals before republicans, and most austerely contemned their radical vices; who, above all, has wasted himself in most generous but most burdensome service to his kind. Any one with a clear vision of essentials in morals will be ready to pronounce that Whitman's loving and patient work in the hospitals through the years of the war is, with his books, sufficient attestation that he is of the salt of his people; and that whether or not all his propositions in sociology be tenable, it is simply absurd to pronounce him a force of evil. Among those who

* He was turned out of the Interior Department at Washington in 1865 by Mr. Harlan for writing "Leaves of Grass." See his article, "An Indian Bureau Reminiscence," in the English Magazine *To-day* for May 1884.

would excommunicate him, it is safe to say, there are few devoted enough to good works to incur paralysis in voluntary hospital labour. Mrs. Grundy never made a more characteristic exhibition than in her verdict on Whitman. It might have bred cynicism in its subject, and will scarcely fail to do so among his less optimistic appreciators.

Let us, however, close the door for a moment on Mrs. Grundy's respected face, and briefly hear in quiet the case against Whitman and his defence. Extenuating nothing, let us note that Emerson protested as warmly against what he called the bad morals of "Leaves of Grass" as he praised the book's great qualities: and let us confess that one bright writer's dexterous account of the denounced passages as amounting to "mere Biblical plainness" is slightly deceptive. Whitman does more than talk plainly of what society objects to talk of in mixed circles. He is unmarried, and he has indicated views which may be assumed to identify him, so far as their distinctive tenet goes, with those who make light of the marriage tie— a party who, some years ago, seemed to be gaining ground in America, but of late have not been much heard of abroad. This, with perhaps one exception, is from the ordinary point of view the most serious charge which can be made against Whitman. On this head there is but little to say. Whitman has published "A Memorandum at a venture," in which, on Millet's text, "All is proper to be expressed, provided only our aim is high enough," he argues for the view he has adhered to for twenty years, "that the sexual passion in itself, while normal and unperverted, is inherently legitimate, creditable, not necessarily an improper theme for poet, as confessedly not for scientist;" but he says nothing on the marriage question. It is therefore to be presumed that he has not cared to burn his fingers further over a subject on which he sees opinion is almost universally intractable to innovating theories. That recognised, the subject may on the whole judiciously be left alone by his admirers, with the proviso, however, that no Philistine shall be allowed unchallenged to execrate Whitman, while Plato is treated with reverence. It is surely time that religious tolerance should be made to extend to admitting that a man may be a good citizen though he holds theories which, carried out, would work extensive changes in social relations. People profess to believe in evolution, yet treat every new speculation as less an error than a crime. At least let Whitman, his morals in other respects being granted irreproachable, receive from cultured men the tolerance with which they view the domestic transactions of Socrates and the social doctrines of Plato; seeing that to-day, as of old, Aristophanes is among the champions of propriety and use-and-wont. At least let us be above the imbecility exemplified in that moral American legislation which disfranchises the Mormon polygamist, and leaves undisturbed his neighbour who only keeps concubines. British and American society of to-day, with its greasy hypocrisies, can hardly pronounce the last word in such a matter. In point of fact, Whitman has never pressed counsel one way or another on his readers. Even had he speculated explicitly in this direction as in others, he might surely be listened to without shrieks of terror; but there is no reason to believe because of variation on his own part that he does not hold marriage a fundamental institution of the present era, any more than that he expects or desires a speedy attainment of socialism.

A fair-minded reader will more readily take sides against Whitman on the minor ground of his mere "Biblical plainness." Here he can now be heard in his defence, and it is impossible not to credit him with an entire superiority to that mere pruriency which so strangely goes unrebuked in many writers so long as they do but avoid directness, biblical or other.

Whitman had already challenged the reigning morality of his countrymen forcibly enough. "Observe," he says, in one of his 'general notes,' "that the most impudent slanders, low insults, etc. on the great revolutionary authors, leaders, poets, etc. of Europe have their origin and main circulation in certain circles here. The treatment of Victor Hugo living, and of Byron dead, are samples. Both deserving so well of America; and both persistently attempted to be soiled here by unclean birds, male and female." There is, perhaps, something of the wisdom of the serpent in this fashion of carrying the war into the enemy's country, refreshingly parodied of late in Mr. Swinburne's attacks on Carlyle, but no one can pronounce the "memorandum at a venture" other than the dignified deliverance of a high-minded man, who is honestly above that taste for the after-dinner erotic which he can righteously charge on perhaps the majority of his male contemporaries. Whitman's argument is that the real harm lies in the conventional shame to which he attributes "that human pathologic evil and morbidity which is, in my opinion, the keel and reason-why of every evil and morbidity." "Its scent," he adds, "as of something sneaking, furtive, and mephitic, seems to lingeringly pervade all modern literature, conversation, and manners."

Now, though it may not be apparent at first, the

conflict here between Whitman and those who gainsay him is really one between optimism and pessimism. Theism is essentially optimistic, and those who protest against Whitman's freedoms are usually theists; but it is not easy to see how they can philosophically justify at once their agreements with him and their dissent. It may be suspected that they seldom try. The ordinary optimist pronounces all things, sin apart, good in their place, but proceeds to snub certain of the unblamed tendencies and phenomena as little better than necessary evils. He cannot in fact get rid of the inheritance of pessimism which comes down with the Christian legend; he still hangs his head in sympathy with Adam and Eve. Whitman comes about as near being a consistent optimist as any man well can, being not even put out by sin; and it will be difficult to show that he is not within his rights in claiming that the motive force of the race shall be sung as heartily as the spring, or as motherhood and friendship. He can fairly challenge the professing optimist to choose whether he will or will not renounce Schopenhauer; whether he will expressly repudiate the teaching that humanity is duped by the will-to-live, or give it colour by his attitude.

Emerson seems to have had no suspicion of any flaw in his case when he mixed reprobation of the indecorum of "Leaves of Grass," with eulogy of its wit and wisdom. Whitman gives a curiously interesting account of how, after they first became acquainted, he walked about with Emerson in Boston for two hours of a bright February day, discussing the proprieties.

"Emerson was then in his prime, keen, physically and morally magnetic, arm'd at every point, and when he chose wielding the emotional just as well as the intellectual. During those two hours he was the talker and I the listener. It was an argument—statement, reconnoitring, review, attack, and pressing home (like an army corps in order, artillery, cavalry, and infantry), of all that could be said against that part (and a main part) in the construction of my poems 'Children of Adam.' More precious than gold to me that dissertation—it afforded me, ever after, this strange and paradoxical lesson; each point of E.'s statement was unanswerable, no judge's charge ever more complete or convincing, I could never hear the points better put—and then I felt down in my soul the clear and unmistakeable conviction to disobey all and pursue my own way. 'What have you to say then to such things?' said E., pausing in conclusion. 'Only that while I can't answer them at all, I feel more settled than ever to adhere to my own theory and exemplify it,' was my candid response. Whereupon we went and had a good dinner at the American House. And thenceforward I never wavered or was touched with qualms (as I confess I had been two or three times before)."

From this two things are very apparent; one, that Whitman is essentially poet rather than doctrinaire, though beside other optimist poets like Browning and Hugo he may seem more teacher than singer; the other, that his hostility to conventional modesty springs as directly from his personality as does his democracy. He is the arch-optimist and poet of optimism; and it is certainly meet that he have a hearing.

Far be it from the literary critic to attempt to put either optimism or pessimism on its trial; but let him for the nonce, sheltering under the wing of George Eliot, dub himself meliorist, and inquire whether Whitman's robust frankness be really possible to his generation. It may be assumed that those who care to follow the inquiry are above the narrowness of impugning his rightness of aim and general moral healthiness even though they may resist his doctrine. Once for all, the man who wrote "Leaves of Grass," and "Democratic Vistas;" who charged himself to spread far and wide the dear love of comrades; who includes in his rules for conduct a command to "stand up for the stupid and crazy;" who gave away his superb health in tending wounded men; and who has freely received the love of comrades and common people everywhere, whatever he may have had from the cultured—this man makes for goodness and righteousness, for high thinking and noble life, if any does. Once for all, if he is to be put on trial it is because of his very simplicity and incorruptible single-heartedness; because to his undaunted courage nothing that is genuinely human is unworthy of open avowal. And yet, withal, it is to be feared that few of us can exhort him to persevere. Be it that we are so far pessimists; we cannot in cool blood turn to the ground-plan of humanity in the "Children of Adam" poems, and say it is all so brave and fair that we can sing pæans over it with Whitman. It may well be that the incapacity is but the measure of our shortcoming from a higher state yet to be attained by the race; that one day we shall be seen to have been morbid creatures, organisms unfitted to survive; and that a hygienic and serene humanity will "sing the body electric" as we do the other phenomena of nature. But no good will ever be done by affecting an enthusiasm we have not, and sincere speech in the matter is as much incumbent on us as on Whitman. The verdict of the average liberal thinker, then, is likely to be that the animal man is not a subject on which it is possible to keep up permanently an exalted feeling. Let each put the question to himself; nay, let him put it in the market place, for it can be discussed without offence on the broad ground taken up by Whitman. The problem is this: Is bodily function an inspiring theme? Does the mastication of food, the chemical action of the stomach, chymification and chylification, the functions of heart, kidneys and liver—does any or do all move us to lyric ecstacy? Sing one, sing all; and Whitman catalogues everything, more or less, with his unhappy faculty in that direction. Perhaps after all he could best be answered by a challenge to sing with any measure of afflatus the act of dining, confessedly as necessary as any other human procedure. What he has done is to sing the appetite that associates itself with passion; and the question arises whether after all he is not deceiving himself; whether he is not really inspired by immemorial poetic association of hope and music and joy, rather than by any discovery of worthiness in appetite. Let him sing dinner if he would dispel the doubt. All of us can feel something poetic in the concept of wine; but what we think of is not so much Hochheimer; it is a something from grapes, "tasting of Flora and the country green—dance, and Provençal song, and sunburnt mirth"; an elixir flavoured with southern skies and sunlight, eternal passion, and old-world dreams which are to the race as memories of youth and spring. But who shall sing beer or whisky-straight? There is abundant and authoritative testimony to the fecundity of the States in original and characteristic beverages; but Whitman has somehow omitted them even from his numerous and exhaustive catalogues. There is surely something wrong about the theory of the beauty of appetite.

It still remains to weigh the special charge against Whitman that is based on such poems as that "To a Common Prostitute," "A Woman Waits for Me," and "Native Moments;" and of course after judgment has gone against the poet on the question of the glorification of appetite generally it is sufficiently difficult to say anything in his defence here. Yet we may profitably pause before pronouncing summary sentence, and ask ourselves whether we have no need to obey that formidable injunction of Dr. Johnson to his biographer, "Clear your mind of cant;"—an injunction bestowed pretty much in vain, as was but natural, considering that the giver had himself fallen considerably short of the prescribed standard. How many of us, in the first place, can without prudery or puritanism or false pretences say that the spirit of Whitman's condemned poems is quite alien to us? The question here is not one of poetic method but of moral judgment. Suppose that Whitman be denied any credit for magnanimity: suppose the general answer to be that he has gone below the level of feeling of cultured men—the matter is still not settled. Emerson presumably had this part of the subject in his mind when he vehemently reproached the new poet: suppose even it be decided that Whitman is after all to be convicted of a certain occasional coarseness of feeling, some lack of desirable delicacy being held an inevitable concomitant of such a life as his, with its extensive associations with "powerful uneducated persons." There is, unhappily, some colour for such a judgment not merely in some remarks of Whitman's about the too great stress laid on manners —these need disturb nobody—but in a "Note Left Over," on Emerson, perhaps the most really regrettable thing he has written. He has spoken reverently and well of his dead friend, but in this note, evidently the outcome of a sour mood, he has gone far to unsay his previous tribute. As literary criticism it is bad. That "Emerson is not eminent as poet or artist or teacher, though valuable in all these"—that he is "best as critic or diagnoser"—is one of several literary misjudgments of Whitman's. It is difficult to see anything but perversity in the following:—

"At times it has been doubtful to me if Emerson really knows or feels what poetry is at its highest, as in the Bible, for instance, or Homer, or Shakespeare. I see he covertly or plainly likes best superb verbal polish, or something old or odd. Waller's 'Go, lovely rose,' or Lovelace's lines 'to Lucasta'—the quaint conceits of the old French bards, and the like. Of *power* he seems to have a gentleman's admiration—but in his inmost heart the grandest attribute of God and poets is always subordinate to the octaves, conceits, polite kinks, and verbs."

This in the face of the fact that in the very essay in which Emerson alludes to Waller's "Go, lovely rose," and Lovelace's lines "to Lucasta," he lays down Whitman's own doctrine that "the test or measure of poetic genius is the power to read the poetry of affairs—to fuse the circumstances of to-day; not to use Scott's antique superstitions, or Shakespeare's, but to convert those of the nineteenth century, and of the existing nations, into universal symbols... American life storms about us daily, and is slow to find a tongue... The test of the poet is the power to take the passing day, with its news, its cares, its fears, as he shares them, and hold it up to a divine reason, till he sees it to have a purpose and beauty, and to be related to astronomy and history, and the eternal order of the world."

More jarring still is the observation that "for a philosopher, Emerson possesses a singularly dandified theory of manners," yet more, the conclusion growing out of the discussion of that point:

"The reminiscence that years ago I began like most youngsters to have a touch (though it came late, and was only on the surface) of Emerson-on-the-brain—that I read his writings reverently, and addressed him in print as 'Master,' and for a month or so thought of him as such—I retain not only with composure, but positive satisfaction. I have noticed that most young people of eager minds pass through this stage of exercise."

It is fitting to say here that some of us are content to call Emerson 'Master' still, and that we think Whitman might gracefully have done so to the end; Emerson having prepared many a mind to appreciate, and anticipated not a little of what is best in, his junior; besides giving many a subtle sensation the other does not stir. The note which was *not* left over is just another expression of Whitman's capacity for fanaticism; and here again his fanaticism makes him transgress his own precepts. He has again and again predicted for his country an ideal civilisation; he has even denounced the meanness of its present manners (see p. 18); but when Emerson, too, indicates that the actual is not ideal, the champion of democracy is piqued, and will justify shortcomings because they are characteristically democratic.

But enough of detraction on this head. Granted that Whitman has faults to answer for in respect of delicacy of feeling, it behoves us still to judge him impartially; and we shall have some trouble to censure him emphatically without convicting ourselves of strange lenity to others. Burns and Byron have sung all sorts of amours with comparatively little reproach; Nelson sleeps in St. Paul's; Mr. Browning has justified promiscuity of attachment. But that is not all. Lord Tennyson has sung carnage *con amore;* and if our denunciation of Whitman is to justify itself by an appeal to the higher feelings there must be some protest against the glorification of all lower impulses whatever. There is really no moral difference to the eye of pure reason between the insurgence of elemental passion in "One

Hour to Madness and Joy," and any poem which sympathetically expresses the lust of slaughter. For—to make an end of this part of our study—the reader is in duty bound to make for Whitman the same allowance that he does for Tennyson, namely, that of assuming that the poet is not so much expressing himself as singing a passion which he knows to be human. If Tennyson heartily and persistently experiences the passion of battle which he has sung, he has as much cause to feel shame as Whitman can have. As to " Native Moments," we are doubtless all agreed that the impulse to riot is not one which will bear looking into, but the war spirit being on a similar basis, there is scarcely room for special protest.

Whitman has perhaps himself to thank that his public looks narrowly to the moral bearing of his poetry, and insists rigorously on making him responsible for all it contains; but if the reader will be content to take his every poem as a simple expression of emotion, one thing will speedily be established to the author's advantage, namely, that there is poetic feeling in a greater or less degree in almost all. It might, indeed, be charged against Whitman that he is at times positively carried off his feet by the afflatus—that, morals apart, he at times passes the bounds of sanity, and becomes for us a possessed energumen rather than an inspired truth-singer. This tendency to delirium we must just set against other displays of a leaning to the *banal*, and admit that the latter is only transient. It must be confessed, however, that the most difficult thing of all in judging Whitman is to estimate his purely poetic value. No body of poetry is so difficult to account for or classify on any theory as his. Like the democracy it celebrates, it refuses to conform to old formulas. Whether we say with Johnson that poetry lies in giving an elevated account of things, or with Coleridge, that it is a matter of choice expression, or with Mr Arnold that it is a subtle heightening of phrase and idea—definitions which harmonise obviously enough—Whitman's verse will be found to demand a certain concession for its acceptance. It precipitates the critic on the old paradox which is constantly coming up in all departments of art-criticism, and which is stated in the demand that the <u>artist shall be at once spontaneous and self-controlled, inspired and artificial.</u> The lover of English poetry who comes to Whitman for the first time will probably, in two cases out of three—unless he happens to be familiar with Blake—be merely astonished and irritated, and these sensations some readers never live down. Perhaps the best course for the reader of poetic taste who is capable of appreciating Whitman's ideas is to turn at the first shock from the poetry to the prose. That he is almost sure to find stimulating and rich in suggestion, and when he has thus got into sympathy with the man he will find the poetry much more palatable. At first he will be disposed to insist that there is hardly any difference between the prose and the poetry; that the preface to "Leaves of Grass," dropped into clauses of systematically unequal length, might eke out "American Feuillage" with perfect propriety; that, in short, <u>Whitman simply makes prose pass for poetry by a particular arrangement of type.</u> Though, however, it will be found hardly possible to defend Whitman's artistic method in the long run, that particular criticism will have to be departed from. Taken all over, the verse, hopelessly unrhythmical as it so often seems, **has distinctly** that quality of "lilt," which is after all the generic difference between poetry and prose. It is the difference between walking and running—the nervous tension belonging to the dance—the definition of which as "the poetry of motion" supplies the critic with a really instructive analogy. Add that it is only in his poetry he becomes dramatic or celebrates passion pure and simple, and the distinction between his poetry and his prose is broadly established. But to allow that his verse has poetic quality is one thing; to say it is a successful poetic product is another.

Whitman, who has a decided opinion about poetic expression, would probably accept with Emerson the conception of poetry as having its form originally determined by the pulse-beat and the inhalation and exhalation of the lungs; but to all appearance he refuses to go any further. As in his thinking he takes his stand on primary facts and individual impulse, so in his verse he returns to elementary methods. It may fairly be said to bear to contemporary English poetry some such relation as does an African war-dance to the dances of Europe. The barbarian, like the civilised people in waltz and quadrille, is going through a calculated performance belonging to the domain of art, but his conformity to plan is of the slightest, and delicate precision is entirely beyond him. His excitement is too complete for sustained grace. It is not that the waltzer does not likewise undergo cerebral excitement, but that he attains a more complex form of gratification by planning and timing his motion. In a study of the dances of different ages, by the way, will be found a help to the appreciation of their poetry; the stately constraint of gavotte and minuet having no less clear an affinity to the verse of the last century than have the dreamy languors and reckless movements in the dances of to-day to its poetry—dress in large measure exhibiting the same relation. Whitman, then, has simply reverted to a prior stage of development. The essence of modern poetry may be said to be indicated in Wordsworth's idea of emotion recollected in tranquillity and artistically expressed; while Whitman chafes at the drill, and rejects the artistic pains as belonging to the department of " polite kinks," grammar, and fine manners. And the upshot is that the world is impelled to view Whitman's aversion to graceful poetic form as it does his rejection of manners, and pronounce him a fine specimen of the barbarian. It is worth noting that Blake, much of whose verse is so curiously like Whitman's, likewise gave overt signs of strong leanings to the primitive, his partial insanity being perhaps responsible for such an emphatic exhibition as his appearance in the open air in the garb of Adam.

There is, on the other hand, a danger of being too summary in writing Whitman down a magnificent barbarian in art. A mistaken notion of his culture has been inadvertently fostered in England by Mr. W. M. Rossetti and Mr. Moncure Conway; the former rather unfortunately representing him as having used Emerson's praise to advertise "Leaves of Grass" while entirely unacquainted with Emerson's books; and the latter apparently accepting too unreservedly the poet's remark that his reading was confined mostly to Homer and the Bible. Whitman has since given sketches of his life, from which it appears that at an early age he began to read novels omnivorously; that he did much miscellaneous work in journalism; and that he picked up plenty of general culture, as a receptive American can, without being systematic in his studies. In his later years, it is interesting to observe, he has read more and more; indeed he is rather suspiciously given of late to laying stress on "The Hegelian Formulas," and taking bird's-eye views of literatures, with such results as finding Shakespeare inferior to Æschylus as an exponent of the passions.

"Without being a scientist," he says in his general preface of 1876, "I have thoroughly adopted the conclusions of the great savans and experimentalists of our time, and of the last hundred years, and they have interiorly tinged the chyle of all my verse, for purposes beyond."

Furthermore, he has always loved music. Artistic conformity apart, he has been about as much in the movement of the culture of his time as was Shakespeare. In the very act, then, of diving back to the primitive, such a poet may supply us with the germs of a new artistic growth.

If such there be, they can best be got at by examining some of the finer passages in his poems. Whitmanites, when challenged to produce from his books a piece of real verse, are given with rather amusing unanimity to cite the lines, "O Captain, my Captain!" on the death of Lincoln, which are partly rhymed; but he has done better work in which there is no suggestion of imitation of accepted forms. "President Lincoln's Burial Hymn," for instance, is rhythmic, and more or less beautiful throughout. Thus it begins:—

> When lilacs last in the door-yard bloom'd
> And the great star early droop'd in the western sky in the night,
> I mourned—and yet shall mourn with ever-returning spring.
>
> O ever-returning spring! trinity sure to me you bring;
> Lilac blooming perennial, and drooping star in the west,
> And thought of him I love.

It does not need the half-reluctant praise conceded to Tennyson in the essay on "Poetry to-day in America" to let the reader know that Whitman has read at least portions of "Maud." The same music recurs:—

Sing on! sing on, you grey-brown bird!
Sing from the swamps, the recesses,—pour your chant from the bushes;
Limitless out of the dusk, out of the cedars and pines.

. . . . . .

Then with the knowledge of death as walking one side of me,
And the thought of death close-walking the other side of me,
And I in the middle, as with companions, and as holding the hands of companions,

I fled forth to the hiding receiving night, that talks not,
Down to the shores of the water, the path by the swamp in the dimness,
To the solemn shadowy cedars, and ghostly pines so still.

And the singer so shy to the rest received me;
The gray-brown bird I know, received us comrades three;
And he sang what seem'd the carol of death and a verse for him I love.

From deep secluded recesses,
From the fragrant cedars, and the ghostly pines so still,
Came the carol of the bird.

And the charm of the carol rapt me,
As I held, as if by their hands, my comrades in the night;
And the voice of my spirit tallied the song of the bird.

The close of the Death Carol [*] is perhaps the most

---

[1] So entitled in Whitman's Centennial Edition of his poems. In Messrs. Wilson and M'Cormick's edition (Glasgow 1883), which bears as a whole the old title "Leaves of Grass," the "Burial Hymn" and "Death Carol" read as parts of one poem, under the heading "Memories of President Lincoln."

musical passage he has written, and fine music it surely is :—

Yet each I keep, and all, retrievements out of the night;
The song, the wondrous chant of the gray-brown bird,
And the tallying chant, the echo arous'd in my soul;
With the lustrous and drooping star; with the countenance full of woe;
With the lilac tall and its blossoms of mastering odor;
With the holders holding my hand, nearing the call of the bird.

Comrades mine, and I in the midst, and their memory ever I keep—for the dead I loved so well;
For the sweetest, wisest soul of all my days and lands—and this for his dear sake;
Lilac and star and bird, twined with the chant of my soul,
There in the fragrant pines, and the cedars dusk and dim.

It is important to notice that this delicate and beautiful work, which was published in 1870, was done after the poet had parted with his robust vigour, worn the yoke of weakness and pain, and exchanged for brooding and reading his old ways of free roaming and "inviting his soul." It is a softer pulse that writes, a more cultured brain that muses and chooses its words. If we want gracious music from Whitman it is to what he wrote after the war that we must mainly turn. Take a snatch in which he has not quite reached his latest mellowness and measure.

RECONCILIATION.

Word over all, beautiful as the sky!
Beautiful that war, and all its deeds of carnage, must in time be utterly lost;
That the hands of the sisters Death and Night, incessantly softly wash again, and ever again, this soiled world:

. . . For my enemy is dead—a man divine as myself is dead;
I look where he lies, white-faced and still, in the coffin—I draw near;
I bend down, and touch lightly with my lips the white face in the coffin.

To be sure, there are reversions in the later work, and anticipations in the earlier. Thus we find in "Passage to India," published in 1870, the following sentence set down in all seriousness for a verse:

He was a good fellow, free-mouth'd, quick-temper'd, not bad-looking, able to take his own part, witty, sensitive to a slight, ready with life or death for a friend, fond of women, gambled, ate hearty, drank hearty, had known what it was to be flush, grew low-spirited towards the last, sicken'd, was help'd by a contribution, died, aged forty-one years, and that was his funeral.

In "Walt Whitman"* again, one of the first-published poems, we have such a lyric outburst as this:—

I am he that walks with the tender and growing night;
I call to the earth and sea, half-held by the night.

Press close, bare-bosom'd night! Press close, magnetic, nourishing night!
Night of south winds! night of the large, few stars!
Still, nodding night! mad, naked summer night.

Smile, O voluptuous, cool-breath'd earth,
Earth of the slumbering and liquid trees;
Earth of departed sunset! earth of the mountains, misty-topt!
Earth of the vitreous pour of the full moon, just tinged with blue!
Earth of shine and dark, mottling the tide of the river!
Earth of the limpid gray of clouds, brighter and clearer for my sake!
Far-swooping, elbow'd earth! rich, apple-blossom'd earth!
Smile, for your lover comes!

Prodigal, you have given me love! Therefore I to you give love!
O unspeakable, passionate love!

---

* Called "Song of Myself" in the Glasgow edition. The poet has made many alterations of this kind, and has excised various passages.

But the broad development is obvious. "Walt Whitman" begins thus :—

I celebrate myself;
And what I assume you shall assume;
For every atom belonging to me, as good as belongs to you.

I loafe and invite my soul;
I lean and loafe at my ease, observing a spear of summer grass—

and concludes thus :—

The spotted hawk swoops by and accuses me—he complains of my gab and my loitering.

I too am not a bit tamed—I too am untranslatable;
I sound my barbaric yawp over the roofs of the world.

The last scud of day holds back for me;
It flings my likeness after the rest, and true as any, on the shadow'd wilds;
It coaxes me to the vapour and the dusk.

I depart as air—I shake my white locks at the runaway sun;
I effuse my flesh in eddies, and drift it in lacy jags.

I bequeathe myself to the dirt, to grow from the grass I love;
If you want me again, look for me under your boot-soles.

You will hardly know who I am, or what I mean;
But I shall be good health to you nevertheless,
And filter and fibre your blood.

Failing to fetch me at first, keep encouraged;
Missing me one place, search another;
I stop somewhere, waiting for you.

And every reader of Whitman remembers vividly the remarkable features of the early "Leaves of Grass," the grotesque phraseology, the coined mongrel words, the abrupt transitions, the reckless collocations of parts of speech, the slang, the insupportable catalogues; and withal the irresistible impressiveness of the strange

new personality, with its piercing depth and directness
of speech, its superb celebration of democracy and
individuality, its new song of friendship, and its
unexampled confidence of inspiration. No poet is
more easily divisible into periods. The Whitman of
"Starting from Paumanok" and "Children of Adam"
is the strong man rejoicing in his strength: the writer
of "Eidólons" and the "Prayer of Columbus" is a
worn old man with all his more delicate perceptions
refined by pain and trouble, with all his thinking
deepened, and with a ripe knowledge of death. A
judgment which should deny genuine poetic value to
the mass of the earlier work, with its primeval inspiration, is impossible; but there can be little question
that the crucial test in poetry—the common sense of
readers as to what is perfectly fit to be treasured in the
memory and crooned or conned over like favourite
music—is much less favourable to the first "Leaves of
Grass" than to the later poems. No doubt it will all
live for many a day. In the straggling footnote to
the general preface of 1876, after defining "Leaves of
Grass" as a type-portrait of a physically healthy
personality, he makes for it the claim "not but what
the brawn of LEAVES OF GRASS is, I think, thoroughly
spiritualised everywhere;" which cannot in strict fair-
ness be denied. And in a late poem of a single stanza
he puts the feeling into lofty and moving song.

AFTER AN INTERVAL.

(*Nov.* 22, 1875, *midnight—Saturn and Mars in conjunction*).

After an interval, reading, here in the midnight,
With the great stars looking on—all the stars of Orion looking,
And the silent Pleiades—and the duo looking of Saturn and ruddy
    Mars;

> Pondering, reading my own songs, after a long interval (sorrow
>   and death familiar now),
> Ere closing the book, what pride! what joy! to find them
> Standing so well the test of death and night,
> And the duo of Saturn and Mars!

He had the right to say it: let that be heartily allowed by all to whom he has given high moments and noble vistas. Not soon will that body of new poetry which he has predicted come to make his look unworthy. It is his own teaching, however, that great developments are in store, and supposing we give him all the credit of a new departure, we still cannot miss detecting the crudeness of the beginnings.

The case for Whitman as an innovator might be put thus: that he embodies a movement of artistic expansion which is very discernible in the shape of Wagnerism in music, and which is *à priori* in keeping with and referable to the great advances in knowledge and in the status of mankind effected in the present century. We have outgrown the thought of the poets of eighty years ago; shall we not expand their forms? Whitman raises the question for us with sufficient definiteness in one of his notes, headed NEW POETRY.

> "For the most cogent purposes of those great inland states [of the future], and for Texas and California and Oregon (and also for universal reasons and purposes, which I will not stop to particularise), in my opinion the time has arrived to essentially break down the barriers of form between Prose and Poetry. I say the latter is henceforth to win and maintain its character, regardless of rhyme, and the measurement rules of iambic, spondee, dactyl, etc., and that even if rhyme and those measurements continue to furnish the medium for inferior writers and themes (especially for persiflage and the comic, as there seems henceforward to the perfect taste, something inevitably comic in rhyme, merely in itself, and anyhow), the truest and greatest POETRY (while subtly and necessarily always

rhythmic and distinguishable easily enough), can never again, in the English language, be express'd in arbitrary and rhyming metre any more than the greatest eloquence, or the truest power and passion. . . . In my opinion, I say, while admitting that the venerable and heavenly forms of chiming versification have in their time play'd great and fitting parts—that the pensive complaint, the ballads, wars, amours, legends of Europe, etc., have, many of them, been inimitably render'd in rhyming verse—that there have been very illustrious poets whose shapes the mantle of such verse has beautifully and appropriately envelopt—and though the mantle has fallen with, perhaps, added beauty on some of our own age—it is, notwithstanding, certain to me, that the day of such conventional rhyme is ended. In America, at any rate, and as a medium of highest esthetic practical or spiritual expression, present or future, it palpably fails, and must fail, to serve. The Muse of the Prairies, and of the peaks of Colorado, dismissing the literary as well as social etiquette of over-sea feudalism and caste, joyfully enlarging, adapting itself to comprehend the size of the whole people, with the free play, emotions, pride, passions, experiences, that belong to them, body and soul—to the general globe, and all its relations in astronomy, as the savans portray them to us—to the modern, the busy nineteenth century (as grandly poetic as any, only different), with steamships, railroads, factories, electric telegraphs, cylinder presses—to the thought of the solidarity of nations, the brotherhood and sisterhood of the entire earth. To the dignity and heroism of the practical labour of farms, factories, foundries, workshops, mines, or on shipboards or on lakes and rivers—resumes that other medium of expression, more flexible, more eligible—soars to the freer, vast, diviner heaven of Prose."

One is driven to ask, after desparately grappling for the syntax, whether the coming Prose is to be such as this. The verdict on Whitman might be arrived at summarily, on his own hint, his avowed prose being distinctly faulty, as many of the foregoing extracts show. Generally vigorous, and terse in respect of its parts, it is yet often slovenly, straggling, and involved —the style of a man who has strong convictions and generally clear ideas, but who will not undergo the drudgery of castigating his language; who, in short, lacks artistic patience. An opinion in favour of rhythmic prose by a writer who writes ordinary prose faultily, and whose own rhythmical writing is frequently harsh, may fairly be received with some suspicion. As for the depreciation of rhyme, that, too, seems largely referable to an incapacity or indisposition to take pains, but the point is one in regard to which we should be careful to avoid bigotry. Let us try to make the hypothesis that we may be listening to a new doctrine which will one day triumph, and ask what are its rational recommendations. Whitman simply pronounces rhyme off hand to be "inevitably comic," and a "medium for inferior writers and inferior themes;" a somewhat courageous declaration, considering how much fun the critics have had over "Leaves of Grass," and how often its style has been parodied. From any point of view whatever, the assertion seems on consideration to be unwarrantably sweeping. The rhythmical "prose" Whitman desires may be presumed to be substantially poetry like his own, though he seems to include all metres in his anathema of rhyme; since he speaks of a poetry which shall be easily distinguishable from common prose. But he has not paused to give a single reason as to why poetry is always "subtly and necessarily rhythmic." Emerson, in his admirable essay on "Poetry and Imagination," which Whitman appears to have read, puts rhyme on the same footing with rhythm as the gratification of a natural taste, subtly suggesting that all things become more beautiful by being reflected in water, the reflection being a rhyme to the eye; that "shadows please us as still finer rhymes;" and that "architecture gives the like pleasure by the repetition of equal parts in a row of windows, or in wings." He detects the same species of charm in a bridal company, a funeral procession, and a row of soldiers. If we try to find reasons for Whitman, we may argue on the superiority of a natural landscape to a garden; but the answer is that we find the same degree of difference between fine and flat poetry—between "Maud," or "The Flight of the Duchess," and "The Borough," or "London"—as between the garden and the landscape. Mere dicta settle nothing. Milton also slighted rhyme; but since Milton, some of the most perfect rhymed poetry in the language has been produced; and none of us are led to reject "Lycidas" or "L'Allegro" by reason of our appreciation of "Paradise Lost." It may very readily be conceded that rhyme grows wearisome in an epic; and that Milton's tale would probably have sounded poorly enough in heroic couplets. That reflection, however, raises another proposition which it would be worth Whitman's while to ponder—and to which, indeed, his own practice in great measure squares, his long pieces being really bundles of short poems—the thesis of Poe, namely, that no poem can far exceed two hundred lines in length and remain perfect. Is it not just as probable that all long poems, blank verse or otherwise, will follow the epic, now admittedly dead, as that rhyme will be relegated to the comic papers? Is not the highest poetry necessarily an affair of brief and concentrated feeling, with expression to correspond; and can we say that we should prefer to have our favourite passages taken out of rhyme and left merely rhythmical? There is no getting over the suspicion that if Whitman had had Tennyson's art, his sense of the comicality of rhyme would never have been developed. His own early scraps of rhyming verse, which he has been compelled to reprint, show no great facility. We may partly sum up in saying that rhyme must in future be much more artistically managed than it is in much work signed with great names; but that there is yet no conclusive reason to suppose art will not keep pace with the demands on it. To-day we find Shelley's Ode to the Skylark slatternly to a distressing degree; and even detect abject puerility in the shifts to which Mr. Browning resorts at times for a rhyme; but Whitman and all his school—if he has a school for his artistic theory—may be challenged to find a single rhyme in, say, Tennyson's stanza:

"Cold and clear-cut face, why come you so cruelly meek?"

that will ring false beside even the closing stanza of the "Death Carol," before quoted; and if they will put the couplet

"Till the war-drum throbb'd no longer, and the battle flags were furl'd
In the Parliament of man, the Federation of the world,"

(where the poet has ventured on a rhyme that is perilously hackneyed), beside any passage from "Beat, Beat Drums," or any similar sentiment from Whitman, they may get some idea of what rhyme can do—some conception of the truth of Hugo's remark, endorsed by Emerson, that "an idea steeped in verse becomes suddenly more incisive and more brilliant; the iron becomes steel." But Whitman's allegation that Tennyson has not written a single democratic line suggests that he has omitted to read some of the most perfect of modern rhymed poetry.

To perverse sayings about the inferiority of rhyme, it can promptly be retorted that rhythm has nothing better to say for itself. Every one of us must sometimes, in a ratiocinating mood, have felt wonder at the act of singing; and the only conclusion possible is that that act and sustained rhythm and rhyme, and dancing, ay, and laughter, are the outcome of a kind of "fine madness," to make an end of which is to take the moonlight out of life. It is scarcely worth any one's while to insist on the special value of prose in the days of Ruskin, and Carlyle, and George Eliot. Coleridge said practically everything on that head in his fragment on the wonderfulness of prose, in which he pictures the charmed surprise of those who, accustomed only to the short recurring cadence of primitive verse, first heard the evolving roll of an orator's sentence. Carlyle, bantering a friend about the passion for putting the accusative before the verb, may be as easily answered as Whitman by a *tu quoque*, with the addition that inversion is no more absolutely necessary in verse than in prose. In fine, most of us will elect to say with Emerson: "I know what you say of mediæval barbarism and sleigh-bell rhyme, but we have not done with music, no, nor with rhyme, nor must console ourselves with prose poets so long as boys whistle and girls sing. Let poetry pass, if it will, into music and rhyme. That is the form which itself puts on." We cling to our verse as we cling to our humour, which also fails to find favour with Whitman.

To that somewhat crude argument that the songs of a wide country require, as it were, long lines, there are many answers, if any one cares to carry the discussion further. Whitman has himself indicated one answer in his general preface:

"Human thought, poetry or melody, must leave dim escapes and outlets—must possess a certain fluid, ærial character; akin to space itself, obscure to those of little or no imagination, but indispensable to the highest purposes. Poetic style, when addressed to the soul, is less definite form, outline, sculpture, and becomes vista, music, half-tints, and even less than half-tints. True, it may be architecture; but again it may be the forest wild-wood, or the best effects thereof, at twilight, the waving oaks and cedars in the wind, and the impalpable odor."

Now this is a very clear expression of a main truth about modern poetry. It is becoming more and more rich in complexities, and it runs more and more to concise treatment; it does not demand great frames and canvases; it seeks subtle condensations and essences, Pisgah-sights, mood-visions, raptures, sighs, and elusive ideas. Does this mean garrulity, and sentences that run on anyhow? The very reverse. No need to reproach Whitman with his cataloguing; even he must long ere this have seen that that was a cheap art method—vivid and stimulating though one or two of his panoramas be. "La concision imagée," says some one, "voilà le style." And rhyme not only lends itself to but demands concision. It is, in fact, a complexity added to rhythm, and therefore, it may be argued, a more finished expression of complex feeling. Our poets will in future assuredly sing less, because all their work must be a more complex product. They too must become specialists. Whitman has himself warned them, in perverse phrase enough:

To oratists—to male or female,
Vocalism, measure, concentration, determination, and the divine
    power to use words.
Are you full-lunged and limber-lipped from long trial? from vigorous
    practice, from physique?
Do you move in these broad lands as broad as they?
Come duly to the divine power to use words?

    For only at last, after many years . . . . it is just possible there comes to a man, a woman, the divine power to use words.

There was surely some self-judgment in the thought, carelessly worded as the demand for art in speech happens to be

On the other hand, while resisting the repudiation of the tried forms as outworn, the unbigoted critic must confess that the movement of expansion promises to do a service not readily to be calculated; and that though the rhymers may hold their own, they must acknowledge the status of singers who can sound the large music of Whitman's best work. He is, indeed, not alone in his departure from the accepted forms; Clough and Arnold, to mention no others, having cast about them—certainly much less boldly—for a more elastic medium than either rhyme or the orthodox blank verse, with notable results. Contemporaneously, Browning and Tennyson have been roaming free in rhyming verse-forms; the former, following Hugo, delighting in intricacies and difficulties; the latter, though much the more careful artist, choosing simpler and looser metres. It is yet too soon to attempt to estimate the respective influence of these various experiments, but their tendency is obvious; and in regard to Whitman's product in particular it is warrantable to say that there is a quality of breadth and fulness in some of it which moves the sensibilities as potently as do its teachings, and which is equally premonitory of coming developments. Precedent and training interfere grievously with our power to appreciate new notes and styles in song; but the sensation Whitman has produced among responsive readers is, on the whole, unequivocal.

Perhaps a more important question than the form of the poetry of the future is that as to the poets' themes and the value that will be set on their work;

but in that direction the inquiry threatens to become endless, swinging round again to the great vista of democracy. It is noteworthy that Whitman gives contradictory opinions on the subject of the themes of the future, though he is quite clear as to the loftiness of the poetic status in the times to be. His predominant conception is that the poets will have an assigned function in a sort of Comtist scheme of things, co-operating with "gangs of prophets and Kosmos," in the Whitman terminology; and interpreting gods and Eidólons" "to the modern, to Democracy;" but he concedes in one place that "after the rest is satiated, all interest culminates in the field of persons, and never flags there;" which is partial amends for fanatical handling of Shakespeare. Pessimism would whisper that "the rest is satiated" very soon for most people, and that the appetite of the Democracy for the strong wine of the ideal is sadly small beside Whitman's. But not in taking leave of Walt Whitman should pessimism make itself heard. He stands there in his stricken old age, contemplating with serene, nay, with still glowing eyes, the vast growth of his beloved nation, refusing to despair over its diseases, looking stedfastly to a golden age beyond; the most significant living figure in American literature. The pessimists of Europe, looking with weary eyes across the melancholy main, find in him an antagonist rather harder to dispose of than Victor Hugo. Not even in confessing that his most characteristic and confident poems in the major key were the expression of an exuberant health, will he admit that he saw things otherwise than as they are. A strenuous persistence has dictated one of his latest pieces, striking both in its avowals and its rebound :—

Ah poverties, wincings, and sulky retreats,
Ah you foes that in conflict have overcome me,
(For what is my life or any man's life but a conflict with foes, the old, the incessant war?)
You degradations, you tussle with passions and appetites,
You smarts from dissatisfied friendships, (ah wounds the sharpest of all!)
You toil of painful and choked articulations, you meannesses,
You shallow-tongued talks at tables, my tongue the shallowest of any;)
You broken resolutions, you racking angers, you smothered ennuis!
Ah think not you finally triumph, my real self has yet to come forth,
It shall yet march forth o'ermastering, till all lies beneath me,
It shall yet stand up the soldier of ultimate victory.

There is a deep, quiet pathos about some aspects of his life; but no dirge comes from him.

"I occupy myself," he says in his preface of 1875, writing on his fifty-sixth birthday, "arranging these pages for publication, still envelopt in thoughts of the death two years since of my dear mother, the most perfect and magnetic character, the rarest combination of practical, moral, and spiritual, and the least selfish, of all and any I have ever known—and by me O so much the most deeply loved . . . and also under the physical affliction of a tedious attack of paralysis, obstinately lingering and keeping its hold upon me, and quite suspending all bodily activity and comfort. . . . I see now, much clearer than ever—perhaps these experiences were needed to shew—how much my former poems, the bulk of them, are indeed the expression of health and strength, and sanest, joyfullest life."

There is no bitterness for him in the memory. He holds, it is true, to the belief in a further life; but he had before sung a carol to death with as bold a note as he had sounded for love and joy; and his religious creed is but the expression of the intensity of his vitality, not a superstition at which he clutches for sustenance. Cold looks and words from his countrymen cannot chill him while his heart beats. The preface to "Leaves of Grass" concluded thus:

"The soul of the largest, and wealthiest, and proudest nation may well go half-way to meet that of its poets. The signs are effectual. There is no fear of mistake. If the one is true the other is true. The proof of a poet is that his country absorbs him as affectionately as he has absorbed it."

In the "Collect" the last four sentences are quietly, pathetically, deleted. The rebuff of time is mutely endured—and the message presented still without complaint. So when history callously falsifies his confident prediction that "when the hundredth year of this Union arrives, there will be some Forty to Fifty great States, among them Canada and Cuba," he tranquilly substitutes "Long, long ere the Second Centennial." No defeats can break down his faith. Age cannot wither it, nor custom stale its manifold expression. Looking round on contemporary poetry, English and French, one is led to suspect that much of it will go the way of last generation's theology, and that poets who have spun their philosophies and gospels into vast webs of verse, "laying great bases for eternity," will be found in a century or so to have spent much labour in vain. But the poetry of Whitman, ill-smelted as so much of it is, cataloquial as is so much of his transcription from life, and lacking as his song so often is in music, somehow does not seem thus marked for doom even in respect of his didacticism. And the reason would seem to be not merely that his message is the intense expression of his deepest passion, but that the passion is the very flower of the life of the race thus far, and carries in it the seeds of things to come. He cannot soon be left behind—he has gone so far before.

JOHN ROBERTSON.

CHARLES DARWIN

NATURALIST

O RUGGED sage, strange confidant wert thou
    Of Nature's choice to learn long secret lore,
    Age-baffling riddles answerless before!
Ah, woman-like, she in the end must bow
To patience of pursuit, to constant vow,
    To cunning study, yielding more and more,
    To thy long siege, until the very core
Of her thought showed, invisible till now.

And thou art crowned with measureless acclaim
    The greatest son of Science' brightest day,
To Newton's self at least co-equal fame:
    Nay more, thou art a rock above the seas
Of superstition, and by thee the way
    To a new church is given, and the keys!

MAN'S thought is like Antæus, and must be
    Touched to the ground of Nature to regain
    Fresh force, new impulse, else it would remain
Dead in the grip of strong Authority.
But, once thereon reset, 'tis like a tree,
    Sap-swollen in spring-time : bonds may not restrain ;
    Nor weight repress ; its rootlets rend in twain
Dead stones and walls and rocks resistlessly.

Thine then it was to touch dead thoughts to earth,
    Till of old dreams sprang new philosophies,
        From visions systems, and beneath thy spell
    Swiftly uprose, like magic palaces,—
Thyself half-conscious only of thy worth—
    Calm priest of a tremendous oracle !

CHARLES DARWIN.

AMONG the men who have endeavoured to establish a new or neglected theory, few have been rewarded by more rapid or more complete success than Charles Darwin in his efforts to obtain recognition for his views of the Origin of Species by means of Natural Selection. Few teachers have been regarded with such admiration by their disciples, or treated with so much respect by their opponents. No innovator has had less reason to complain of the indifference of his contemporaries. Round the "Origin of Species," was waged for years the keenest phase of the contest between the followers of science and the adherents of tradition. More than one generation of naturalists have drawn the inspiration of their best work from their enthusiasm for Darwinism. From Darwin's books evolutionary ideas have permeated into all streams of thought, until natural selection, and the struggle for existence are discerned in operation in all the manifestations of life. The theory of the evolution of living beings by gradual modification was not new. Buffon had suggested it as the necessary conclusion to be drawn from a review of the phenomena of the organic world. Dr. Erasmus Darwin had proclaimed it with a power and eloquence due too much to vividness of imagination, and too little to profundity of research.

Lamarck devoted the latter half of his life to advocating the truth of evolution, and of his views as to the causes of the process. In Britain, immediately before the publication of Darwin's arguments, Herbert Spencer had cogently urged the superiority of the hypothesis of evolution over that of special creation. Wells and Matthews had even reached the conception of natural selection. Yet the great majority of biologists were completely indifferent to these attempts to introduce a new leaven into the prevailing system of ideas concerning living beings. In spite of Buffon and Lamarck, Erasmus Darwin and Herbert Spencer, the greater number of naturalists still pursued their studies with the belief in the immutability of species as the background of their thoughts, and few conceived the possibility of treating as a scientific problem the question whether species were constant or plastic. One or two only, like Wallace, had reached conclusions similar to those of Darwin, and were prepared to support his arguments as soon as he produced them. But in a very short time after the appearance of the "Origin of Species," almost every naturalist of eminence had expressed his conviction of the truth of the conclusions expressed in that book. To Darwin clearly belongs the honour of having finally overthrown the dogma of the immutability of species, and so opened a broad path to the triumphant progress of biological researches. And it is also clear that the most successful weapon which Darwin wielded was the theory of natural selection. Although in many departments of biology it matters less what may be the cause of evolution than that the truth of descent with modification be apprehended, yet it is evident that the arguments of Herbert Spencer would have had little effect on naturalists, and on men of average intelligence, who were nevertheless completely convinced by Darwin's theory of natural selection. So great and steadfast has been the allegiance of biologists in general to Darwin, that little attempt to criticise or develop his views was for a long time made by those who accepted the truth of organic evolution. Those who denied the modification of species altogether opposed Darwin energetically enough, but they fought against immensely superior forces. Some who were convinced of the truth of organic evolution, and were not personally familiar with biological studies, questioned the all-sufficiency of Darwin's explanation, but were usually met with the reply that only naturalists were competent to examine the question, and that naturalists were satisfied with the efficacy of natural selection. Only recently, now that the controversy between evolutionists and anti-evolutionists has subsided, has an impartial criticism of Darwin's position become possible, and the progressive development of the doctrine of organic evolution is now rapidly proceeding.

The mind's capacity for thinking about a phenomenon depends greatly on the ideas already acquired from those who have thought on it before. The possibility of the continuous modification of organisms had been suggested in a vague way before the time of Buffon; but it is obvious that Buffon received less assistance from predecessors than any of his successors received from him. The facts which most powerfully suggested to the great French naturalist the truth of organic evolution, were those of morphological relationship, of cultivation or domestication, and of geographical distribution. The chief causes of modification, according to Buffon, are temperature and climate, the quality of food and the ills of slavery, by which last he means the conditions to which domesticated organisms are subjected by man. Buffon also drew attention to the selection exerted by man on domesticated animals as a means of perpetuating variations. But although he mentions the great tendency of organisms to increase in numbers, he draws no conclusion concerning natural selection by the struggle for existence. Erasmus Darwin was a disciple of Buffon. His arguments are based on the morphological relations of organisms, and the changes due to domestication; his idea of the cause of modification includes, besides the action of the environment, the effect of function, or, as Charles Darwin called it, use and disuse. Lamarck also was brought to his views by the morphological relations of organisms and the phenomena of domestication. Lamarck's idea of the cause of modification is as follows: the environment affects the habits of the animal, and the habits or functions affect the organs, and thus in the course of generations modifications of any extent are produced. Charles Darwin was early acquainted with the works of Buffon, Dr. Darwin and Lamarck, and thus his mind was ready as soon as his interest in living beings was excited, to consider their relation to the doctrine of evolution. At the same time it is evident that Darwin had more respect for the traditional and semi-religious belief in the immutability of species than he had for the earlier evolutionists.

In the 'Journal' he makes mention of Lamarck in discussing the blindness of the Brazilian Tucutuco. "Considering the strictly subterranean habits of the

Tucutuco, the blindness, though so common, cannot be a very serious evil; yet it appears strange that any animal should possess an organ frequently subject to be injured. Lamarck would have been delighted with this fact had he known it when speculating (probably with more truth than usual with him) on the gradually acquired blindness of the Aspalax, a gnawer living underground, and of the Proteus, a reptile living in dark caverns filled with water, in both of which animals the eye is in an almost rudimentary state. . . . No doubt Lamarck would have said that the Tucutuco is now passing into the state of the Aspalax and Proteus." Darwin himself in later years would have said much the same, only he would doubtless have sought to find how the Tucutuco derived some advantage, direct or indirect, from its imperfect vision. Yet his somewhat contemptuous parenthesis shows that at the period of his Journal he rejected altogether the general views of Lamarck, and when years afterwards he expounded his own theory of organic evolution in the "Origin of Species," he referred to the "erroneous views and grounds of opinion of Lamarck." But whatever the young naturalist thought of Lamarck's system, his remarks on the Tucutuco afford only one of the many evidences that his interest in the question of modification *versus* constancy in organic structure was thoroughly aroused during his years of travel. His celebrated chapter on the Galapagos Islands shows us that the probability of mutability in species was presented to him much more distinctly by the facts of distribution than by examples of imperfect adaptation to conditions. The islands are evidently geologically new, raised within a comparatively recent period above the surface of the ocean. Hardly any of the species found in the Archipelago occur in any other part of the world, and there are many species which are confined to a single island. At the same time the species in almost all cases belong to American *genera*.

"It is probable that the islands of the Cape de Verd group resemble in their physical conditions far more closely the Galapagos Islands than these latter physically resemble the coast of America, yet the aboriginal inhabitants of the two groups are totally unlike, those of the Cape de Verd Islands bearing the impress of Africa as those of the Galapagos Archipelago are stamped with that of America." Another series of facts had also brought Darwin near to the problem of the origin of species, namely, the similarity between the fossil and living animals on the same continent. In America "there are fossil ant-eaters, armadilloes, tapirs, peccaries, guanacoes, opossums, and numerous South American gnawers, monkeys and other animals. This wonderful relationship in the same continent between the dead and the living will, I do not doubt, hereafter throw more light on the appearance of organic beings on our earth, and on their disappearance from it than any other class of facts." He mentions Buffon in this connection. "If Buffon had known of the gigantic sloth and armadillo-like animals, and of the later pachydermata, he might have said with a greater semblance of truth that the creative force in America had lost its power rather than that it had never possessed greater power." A little further on he shows that he had at the time of the publication of the Journal considered the subject of the struggle for existence :—" The supply of food on an average remains constant ; yet the tendency in every animal to increase by propagation is geometrical, and its surprising effects have nowhere been more astonishingly shown than in the case of the European animals run wild during the last few centuries in America."

But the greater proportion of his interest and energy was devoted during his voyage to the study of geology. His power and the bent of his mind were abundantly exhibited in this early work. He has the most masterly grasp of detail ; but this faculty is treated not as an end in itself, but as a means of supporting some sweeping generalization, which explains and holds together all the separate phenomena. In the first paper he published after his return from his voyage, he unites all the results of his studies of volcanoes into a comprehensive view of their relation to the elevation of mountain chains. His great work on Coral Islands, published four years afterwards, traces all their features to the continuous subsidence of a portion of the earth's crust, in relation to the habits of coral polyps and the configuration of the portion of land gradually sinking below the sea. For ten years after his return to England, from 1836 to 1846, Darwin was almost entirely devoted to geology. Through these studies he became a firm believer in evolution as the true character of the history of the earth, and the immensity of time, which even small epochs of this history had occupied, was deeply impressed on his mind. We know from his own words that, in spite of his labours in geology, he had the problem of evolution in the world of living things continually in his thoughts. In his introduction to the "Origin of Species," we are told that though facts in the distribution of the organic beings in South America, and of the relation of the living to the fossil inhabitants of that continent, first led him to believe in the possibility of the evolution of living beings through descent with modification, he was not satisfied with believing in the truth of the theory, and supporting it by the facts of embryology, geographical distribution, geological succession, and the analogy of domestic productions. What he required was a cause. Darwin had his own peculiar view of the nature of a cause. He sought some one universal principle which would explain all the details; at least he wanted to have some idea of how the divergence at present existing could have been produced. He rejected entirely, as we have seen, the views of Lamarck. In his letter to Hæckel explaining the course by which he reached his views, he says:—

"At an early period it seemed to me probable that allied species were descended from a common ancestor. But during several years I could not conceive how each form could have been modified so as to become so admirably adapted to its place in nature. I began, therefore, to study domesticated animals and cultivated plants, and after a time perceived that man's power of selecting and breeding from certain individuals was the most powerful of all means in the production of new races. Having attended to the habits of animals and their relations to the surrounding conditions, I was able to realize the severe struggle for existence to which all organisms are subjected; and my geological observations had allowed me to appreciate, to a certain extent, the duration of past geological periods. With my mind thus prepared, I fortunately happened to read Malthus's 'Essay on Population,' and the idea of natural selection through the struggle for existence at once occurred to me. Of all the subordinate points in the theory, the last which I understood was the cause of the tendency, in the descendants from a common progenitor, to diverge in character."

Darwin does not tell us at what period of his mental development he read Malthus. We know the date at which his first manuscript on the subject of natural selection was drawn up. This happened in the year 1839, and the essay was copied in 1844 when the copy was read by Dr. Hooker, and communicated to Sir Charles Lyell. An extract from this manuscript was read before the Linnæan Society in 1858, and published in 1859. This extract develops Darwin's own personal view of the theory of natural selection, in the form in which he held it, with little if any modification, to the end of his life. In the following few sentences the central point of the theory is asserted.

"Now can it be doubted, from the struggle each individual has to obtain subsistence, that any minute variation in structure, habits, or instincts, adapting that individual better to the new conditions, would tell upon its vigour and health? In the struggle it would have a better chance of surviving; and those of its offspring which inherited the variation, be it ever so slight, would also have a better chance. Yearly more are bred than can survive; the smallest grain in the balance in the long run must tell on which death shall fall and which shall survive. Let this work of selection on the one hand and death on the other go on for a thousand generations, who will pretend to affirm that it would produce no effect, when we remember what in a few years Bakewell effected in cattle and Western in sheep, by this identical principle of selection."

In this published extract, as in all his expositions of his views, Darwin does not neglect the question of the origin of variations, but he does not go into it very elaborately. In the published extract, only half a paragraph deals with this question.

"Let the internal conditions of a country alter," he says, "if in a small degree, the relative proportions of the inhabitants will, in most cases, simply be slightly changed; but let the number of inhabitants be small, as on an island, and free access to it from other countries be circumscribed, and let the change of conditions be circumscribed (forming new stations), in such a case the original inhabitants must cease to be as perfectly adapted to the changed conditions as they were originally. It has been shown in a former part of this work that such changes of external conditions would, from their acting on the reproductive system, probably cause the organization of those beings which were most affected to become, as under domestication, plastic."

Let us turn over the pages of the "Origin of Species," and see how the discussion of the problem is there elaborated. In the introduction it is pointed out that an unprejudiced naturalist, reflecting on various kinds of facts concerning organisms—such as their mutual affinities, by which is meant their morphological resemblances and differences; their embryological relations, the appearance, in the embryo, of structures which must once have been of use in a kind of life very different to that of the adult; their geographical distribution, as in the instance of the Galapagos Islands; and their geological succession, such as fossil sloths in South America, very different from the existing forms—might come to the conclusion that each species had not been independently created, but had descended like varieties from other species. Nevertheless, such a conclusion would be unsatisfactory, unless it could be shown *how* the innumerable species inhabiting this world have been modified so as to acquire that perfection of structure and co-adaptation which justly excites our admiration.

Naturalists continually refer to external conditions, such as climate, food, etc., as the only possible cause of variation. In one limited sense, this may be true; but it is preposterous to attribute to mere external conditions the structure, for instance, of the woodpecker, with its feet, tail, beak and tongue so admirably adapted to catch insects under the bark of trees. It is equally preposterous to account for the structure of the mistletoe, with its relation to several distinct organic beings, by the effects of external conditions, or of habit, or of the volition of the plant itself. It is therefore of the highest importance to gain a clear insight into the means of modification and co-adaptation. To do this the author studies domesticated animals and cultivated plants.

First of all are considered the causes of variability, which, as we shall have occasion to suggest later, are as much in want of investigation now as when the "Origin of Species" was published. Cultivated organisms are more variable than those in nature: there is more difference between two individuals of a cultivated rose, than between two of the wild rose, and more difference between any two English racehorses than between any two zebras. The cause of this we are driven to conclude, is that the domesticated organisms have been raised under conditions of life not so uniform, and somewhat different from those to which the parent species had been exposed under nature. Some change is effected by the direct action of new conditions: that is, each generation, *as a whole*, not only some individuals, is changed from the parents in a certain direction. This is definite variability. The several breeds of the pigeon differ more than natural species from one another; yet it is almost certain that they are all descended from the rock-pigeon, *Columba livia*. But in the formation of all domesticated breeds the principal cause has been human selection; each breed possesses characters which in some special way serve man's wants or pleasures: and the breed has been produced by man, selecting in each generation among the varying individuals those in which such characters were present in the greatest degree.

The next question is, do variations occur in a state of nature; and the answer is that no two individuals of a given species are exactly alike. Any naturalist who examines a number of specimens of one species finds in some the "specific characters" all well marked, in others all of them less pronounced, while in others some are distinct, others less prominent. In many species there exist *varieties* which only differ from *species* in diverging in a less degree from the species to which they belong, and by being united to them by intermediate links in which the characters of the variety and the species are blended.

But the mere existence of individual variability, and of some few well-marked varieties is not sufficient to account for the exquisite adaptions of one part of the organization to another part, and to the conditions of life. Nor does it explain how varieties become converted into distinct species, and how the groups of species known as *genera* arise. These results follow from the struggle for life. Owing to this struggle, variations, however slight and from whatever cause proceeding, if they be in any degree profitable to the individuals of a species, in their infinitely complex relations to other organic beings, and to their physical conditions of life, will tend to the preservation of such individuals, and will generally be inherited by the offspring. This is the principle of Natural Selection, called by Herbert Spencer, "the survival of the fittest." Darwin points out that the term, "struggle for existence," is used in a large and metaphorical sense. The struggle inevitably follows from the high rate at which all organic beings tend to increase, while the actual numbers of a given species never increase so fast, often decrease, and sometimes remain stationary. There is no exception to the rule that every organic being naturally increases at so high a rate, that, if not destroyed, the earth would soon be covered by the progeny of a single pair. Even slow-breeding man has doubled in twenty-five years, and at this rate in less than a thousand years there would literally not be standing room for his progeny. There is direct evidence of the high rate of increase in numerous instances. The cattle and horses introduced into South America, and latterly into Australia, have multiplied to an enormous extent, and this not because the rate of breeding has increased, but because the conditions were favourable, principally because suitable food was abundant. The exact nature of the checks to increase, of the conditions which limit the population of a given species, is obscure. The amount of food gives the extreme limit, but very frequently it is more the danger from enemies in the shape of other organisms which restricts the numbers. The complex relations in which animals and plants stand to one another when the subject is examined are seen to be marvellous. The celebrated instance given by Darwin may here be quoted :—Red clover, Trifolium protense, can only be fertilized by humble bees. The number of humble bees depends in great measure on the number of field-mice, which destroy their combs and nests, and the number of field-mice is largely dependent on the number of cats.

Carl Vogt has pursued this chain of argument a little further. "As the red clover is one of the most important and best foods for the bullock, its quantity and quality influences the quantity and quality of beef, which is well known to be indispensable for the proper nourishment of the British nation. As further the most highly developed functions of this nation, its industry, marine, free institutions depend on the strong development of the brains of Britons, which again depends on the abundant nourishment of these brains with beef, we find that the number of cats in England has ultimately a profound influence on the whole perfection of culture, which at the present time places Britain in many respects at the head of all nations."

The most difficult thing to understand, according to Darwin, is how divergence of character is produced, or when produced tends to increase. The explanation is that the greatest amount of life can be supported by greatest diversification of structure. A carnivorous quadruped can only succeed in increasing by its varying descendants seizing on places at present occupied by other animals, some inhabiting new stations, climbing trees, frequenting water, and some perhaps becoming less carnivorous.

By natural selection, each creature tends to become more and more improved in relation to its conditions, and then Darwin goes on to say this improvement inevitably leads to the gradual advancement of the organization of the greater number of living beings throughout the world. If we take as the standard of high organization, the amount of differentiation and specialization of the several organs in each being when adult natural selection clearly leads towards this standard; for all physiologists admit that the specialization of organs is an advantage to each being. But it is quite possible for natural selection gradually to fit a being to a situation in which several organs would be superfluous or useless.

The next chapter discusses the laws of variation, which are generalizations based on a survey of facts, though the actual causes of variation are not very evident. Use and disuse of parts have caused the greater development or the reduction of these parts. Homologous parts tend to vary in the same manner, and when adjacent, tend to cohere. Organic beings low in the scale are more variable than those standing higher. Rudimentary organs are variable.

The existence of lowly organized forms is briefly discussed:—

> "In some cases lowly organized forms appear to have been preserved to the present day from inhabiting confined or peculiar stations, where they have been subjected to less severe competition, and where their scanty numbers have retarded the chance of favourable variations arising. In some cases, variations or individual differences of a favourable nature may never have arisen for natural selection to act on and accumulate. In some few cases there has been what we must call retrogression of organization. But the main cause lies in the fact that under very simple conditions of life, a high organization would be of no service—possibly would be of actual disservice, as being of a more delicate nature and more liable to be put out of order and injured."

The difficulties of the theory are frankly considered. The chief of these are the absence of transitions, the existence of instincts and organs of extreme complexity, and the fact that species when crossed are either sterile or produce sterile offspring, whereas varieties when crossed breed with unimpaired fertility. It is shown that instincts, however originally acquired, are inherited, and are variable; hence they are liable to be improved and specialized by natural selection.

Another great objection to the acceptance of the theory of evolution is the absence of intermediate links among fossil forms, but Darwin shows that the geological record is necessarily very imperfect, and the intermediate links, which do exist among fossil forms, cannot be accounted for at all on any other hypothesis than that of descent with modification.

The phenomena of geographical distribution are next reviewed, and the impossibility of accounting for them on any other hypothesis than that of evolution insisted upon. Finally, the classification of organisms, the facts of embryology and morphology are reviewed, and all shown to support the theory. The arguments drawn from these various departments of biological science are not essentially different in Darwin's hands from what they were when treated by his predecessors. But since the time of Lamarck, knowledge in these departments had enormously increased, especially in that of embryology. Darwin presented the mass of evidence with a force derived from the breadth and diversity of his knowledge; and it may be said that these arguments give the momentum to his demonstration, while the point of the instrument is furnished by his theory of the method of evolution.

Darwin considered the "Origin of Species" as only a general sketch of this theory and the facts which support it. He originally intended to treat each one of its chapters in greater detail, and so expand it into a volume. This plan was never carried out to the letter; the volumes on the variation of animals and plants under domestication appeared, but the proposed works on variation of organisms in a state of nature, on the struggle for existence and natural selection were never written. Their place was supplied by the succession of works, describing beautiful and elaborate researches into the most diverse classes of biological phenomena, which will ever remain among the classics of the literature of science. Some of these volumes are monuments rather of bibliographical than empirical inquiry: they all have a close relation to the question of organic evolution, but they do not describe investigations into the process of modification, into the causes of variation or of heredity. They enlarge the boundaries of knowledge, and bring into the field of mental vision new phenomena to be explained by the general theory of biology. Darwin acknowledged that his explanation of organic evolution was not exhaustive, but he devoted himself to the application of the theory he had adopted rather than to the deeper investigation of the premises on which it was based. He had no other choice; he was not a specialist in physiological studies, and even if he had been, the physiology of his day could have given him little guidance. In its present state physiology can say little definite on the fundamental problems of heredity and variation, they remain to be attacked by the physiology of the future.

The two volumes on the "Variation of Animals and Plants under Domestication" were published in 1868. In this case, the original intention to publish a detailed examination of each class of facts embraced in the theory of natural selection was completely carried out; we have a study as exhaustive as the wonderful working power of Darwin could make it, of the process of modification which can be actually traced in the history of cultivated forms of life. In the introduction the whole theory of evolution is restated in outline. The links in the argument are very much what they were before. Man unintentionally exposes his animals and plants to various conditions of life, and variability supervenes, which he cannot prevent or check. The variations are inherited, and by selecting certain variations to propagate from, man is able to modify species in almost any direction he pleases. Similarly, variations undoubtedly occur in a state of nature, and only those in which the variation is an improvement in relation to the conditions of life, being able to survive, natural selection produces modification and divergence. The first volume is simply and solely a collection of facts; it describes the variations which have occurred in cultivated organisms, and the effects which have been produced by selecting the variations. In the second volume we have a study of the phenomena of inheritance, selection, the causes of variation, and the laws of variation. In the chapter on the causes of variation, it is distinctly explained that "variations of all kinds and degrees are directly or indirectly caused by the conditions of life to which each being, and more especially its ancestors, have been exposed." Use and disuse are shown to be important causes of modification, by increasing or decreasing an organ; the structure of an organ changes when the use of it, that is to say, its function, changes.

In this work, Darwin attempted to penetrate the mystery of the process of heredity by the light of imagination. It contains his hypothesis of pangenesis. Here for once he deserted his usual method of proceeding always from the known to the unknown, from the familiar to the apparently inexplicable. His gemmules have no relation to any known facts concerning the structure or functions of organisms. The reproductive elements are known to be unspecialized cells which are nourished, like the rest of the cells in the organism, by the circulating fluids. We know that the reproductive cells have the property of going through the same series of changes as those exhibited by the parent, and we know that this property must have been impressed upon them in some way or other while in the body of the parent. But our knowledge is not made clearer by a hypothesis of gemmules which build up the reproductive cells. It is certain that the cells are not built up by composition from smaller units, unless the supposed units are the molecules of the substances by which the reproductive cells are nourished.

The "Fertilization of Orchids" preceded "Animals and Plants under Domestication," although it has less immediate connection with the doctrine of evolution. To the general reader it is perhaps the most attractive of all Darwin's works. The investigation of the way in which cross-fertilization is effected in the orchids might have been carried out without a belief in evolution. The point of view from which Darwin regards the subject is easily indicated. It is a fact, though we do not know exactly why, that cross-fertilization is an advantage to bisexual plants, and every peculiarity in orchidaceous flowers, the simplest as well as the most brizarre and apparently monstrous, has some definite relation to the agencies by which cross-fertilization is effected, that is to say, to the structure and habits of insects, which carry the pollen from one plant to another. Thus in plants originally of the regular form, slight variations arose, by which cross-fertilization was favoured; the offspring of these therefore survived, and were more vigorous than the seedlings of the unmodified flowers, and natural selection thus accumulated the variations until the results we now see were produced. In this work an important principle in the theory of modification is enunciated and illustrated, the principle of change of function, on which so much stress has been laid by Dr. Dohrn, in his inquiries into the probable history of the vertebrate organization :—

"The regular course of events seems to be that a part which

originally served for one purpose, by slow changes becomes adapted for widely different purposes. To give an instance :—In all the Ophreæ, the long and nearly rigid caudicle manifestly serves for the application of the pollen grains to the stigma when the pollinium attached to an insect is transported from flower to flower : and the anther opens widely that the pollinium may be easily withdrawn. But in the Bee Ophrys, the caudicle, by a slight increase in length and decrease in thickness, and by the anther opening a little more widely, becomes specially adapted for the very different purpose of self-fertilization, through the combined aid of the gravity of the pollen and the vibration of the flower."

The lines of inquiry indicated in this work were followed up further some years later in a series of elaborate experiments upon the effects of cross and self-fertilization, which showed that as a matter of actual observation cross-fertilization causes an increased vigour in the offspring of plants in the very first generation. We are still in ignorance of the reason of this ; our understanding of the matter remains very much where Darwin left it.

The "Descent of Man" is a special study of the facts which prove that man's morphological relation to the anthropoid apes is not different in kind to that of any genus to another of the same family. In the "Movements and Habits of Climbing Plants," it was shown that all the motions exhibited by plants are specializations of one universally present movement, that of circumnutation, and that each particular motion could thus be produced by natural selection acting on variations of circumnutation. "Different Forms of Flowers" is a contribution to the subject of adaptations for cross-fertilization in plants. In his last work Darwin returned to a geological subject which has no direct connection with the evolution of organic beings, but is a study of one of the most minute and obscure among geological agencies.

Thus the great naturalist's contribution to the general theory of organic evolution ends with the "Animals and Plants under Domestication," and we return to the study of the arguments and conclusions which have played so important a part in the history of modern thought.

It cannot be maintained that those arguments are always formulated with perfect logical consistency. Examined closely, the conception of natural selection comes to this:—An organism usually possesses the same structure as its parents, or to put it in another way, the progeny of organisms of a given species possess the distinguishing characters of that species, But certain individuals of a species may, from some cause or other, before they begin to reproduce, be slightly altered from the exact specific standard, and this alteration is inherited by their descendants to an indefinite number of generations. If this alteration is such that the individuals affected by it are more perfectly adapted to their conditions of life, they will leave more progeny than the unaltered individuals, and thus the alteration in successive generations is present in an increasingly larger number of individuals. To take a specific instance, if a few of the ancestors of the giraffe were endowed from some cause or other with an increased length of neck and were thus enabled to gain a better living and leave more progeny than their brethren, each successive generation would have more individuals with a longer neck. Every time that an increased length of neck was from some cause or other produced, natural selection would tend to diffuse the advantage over the whole species. That is to say, the species, owing to the struggle for existence, would soon come to consist only of the descendants of those individuals in which some cause had increased the length of the neck. If some cause modified every existing individual of a species exactly to the same extent, natural selection would have absolutely no effect. If some agency caused all the individuals of a species to be less perfectly adapted to their conditions of life, they would soon become extinct, supposing no other conditions of life were open to them. Effects of the kinds thus indicated are the only ones that can follow from natural selection. Natural selection obviously can never be the cause of modification in any given individual. It may, and doubtless does, distribute in a few generations the peculiarities somehow acquired by one or more individuals over a whole species. As this process of picking out modifications goes on in successive generations, any increase in certain individuals of a modification already begun is also distributed over the whole species. This is all that can be meant by the cumulative action of natural selection. But though Darwin sometimes applies to the action of natural selection an analysis as accurate as that attempted above, he frequently attributes to the process effects which are quite beyond its scope.

For example, in discussing compensation and economy of growth, he says:—

"Thus, as I believe, natural selection will tend in the long run to reduce any part of the organization as soon as it becomes through changed habits superfluous, without by any means causing some other part to be largely developed in a corresponding degree. And conversely that natural selection may perfectly well succeed in largely developing an organ without requiring as a necessary compensation the reduction of some adjoining part."

Natural selection can have nothing whatever to do with either the reduction or the development of an organ; it can only ensure that if the reduction or development occur in one or more individuals, and be an advantage in life, the change shall be present in each generation in a proportionally larger number of individuals. Here is another sentence in which the limitations of the action of natural selection are obscured.

"When a variation is of the slightest use to any being, we cannot tell how much to attribute to the accumulative action of natural selection, and how much to the definite action of the conditions of life. Thus it is well known to furriers that animals of the same species have thicker and better fur the further north they live; but who can tell how much of this difference may be due to the warmest clad individuals having been favoured and preserved during many generations, and how much to the action of the severe climate?"

Natural selection must be always acting when the modification of the fur is different in different individuals. The question is, How is the modification produced? If by the action of the climate, then in what way does exposure to a severe climate cause the fur to become thicker? If we take the word environment as including all the possible causes of modification in a given organism, it is impossible to distinguish, as Darwin attempts to do, between changes due to the environment on the one hand, and changes due to natural selection on the other. It is probable that one of the chief causes of modification is increased or diminished function, and the various changes of function are all summed up in the conception of the struggle for existence.

To Darwin the chief importance of the struggle for existence was that it gave rise to natural selection. To the biologist who believes in function as the chief agent in modification and function as a reaction to stimulus, the chief importance of the struggle for existence is its relation to stimulus and function.

Natural selection cannot cause an iota of modification in structure. An important distinction may be drawn between general and particular conditions in the modifying environment. It may be profitable to discover for example the difference between the effects on a species of animals, of an increase of average temperature, and of an increased difficulty in procuring food. The increased temperature would in the case of a mammal increase the amount of perspiration, and so cause a more rapid passage of liquids through the tissues, and modify the rate of circulation; these changes would probably result in structural modification. An increased difficulty in procuring food could, as far as natural selection is concerned, do nothing more than reduce the species to the descendants of the better endowed individuals already existing; in relation to the struggle for existence, it would necessitate the more vigorous exercise of certain functions, and this would doubtless result in an improvement of structure. Professor Weismann has recently denied altogether the inheritance of characters and changes acquired in the life of an individual, and attributes modification to the combination in the offspring of the heritable characters of the two parents which unite for reproduction. Even if this were true, natural selection could not be called the cause of modification, it could only ensure the survival of characters due to the interaction of the heritable qualities of the parents.

In the following sentence, Darwin more clearly defines the mode of action of natural selection:—

"In one sense the conditions of life may be said not only to cause variability directly or indirectly, but likewise to include natural selection; for the conditions determine whether this or that variety shall survive. But when man is the selecting agent, we clearly see that the two elements of change are distinct; variability is in some manner excited, but it is the will of man which accumulates the variations in certain directions: and it is this latter agency which answers to the survival of the fittest under nature."

We have here an instance of the way in which Darwin was enslaved by the spirit he had conjured; he was unable to escape from the anthropomorphism of his own theory. In the case of human selection, not the least modification in an organism can be produced by the process of selection itself. The modifications somehow produced in the animals selected are transmitted to the offspring; but the cause of modification lies elsewhere than in selection; and it is largely due to man's own modification of the environment. In breeding race-horses, training receives at least as much attention as selection; and training is in great measure the application of stimuli to act upon function in the belief that function will modify structure. It is not intended to suggest here that Darwin denied the effect of increased or diminished function; but although he confesses that a complete theory of evolution would include a knowledge of the cause of every variation, he does not devote much attention to the analysis of those causes which he mentions. In considering the process by which Madeira beetles have become wingless, he is inclined to lay far more stress on the fact that the strong-winged individuals in each generation have been blown to sea and destroyed, than on the processes by which the wings of the survivors have been reduced. Undoubtedly in such a case as this, natural selection by the elimination of certain individuals is a most important factor in the rapid modification of a given species. But the question is, can it be called a cause of modification? All that can be allowed is that the process indicated by the term, the destruction of the unfit, has an important influence on the rate at which the character of a species is altered. Natural selection can never help us to understand the causes of variability or of inheritance. No instance illustrates more forcibly the theory of natural selection than that of the Madeira beetles; but suppose that natural selection in this case were so efficient that all the individuals were blown away, then the species would not be evolved, but removed altogether.

This hypothetical example shows the point at which the preceding criticism is directed. The objections raised apply only to Darwin's discussion of the laws and causes of variation in the "Origin of Species;" from which chapter it would undoubtedly have been better had he omitted natural selection as a modifying agent altogether. No such objection can be made to his exposition of the action of natural selection in causing the extinction of a large number of organic forms. Certain conditions, general or particular do not modify an organism or a species, but destroy it, or as the Americanism epigrammatically expresses the fact, "improve it off the face of the earth." Thus, intermediate forms are removed, and intervals of various degrees between groups of living forms produced.

In the "Animals and Plants under Domestication," the error of confusing the process of selection with the causes of variation is entirely avoided. The later work is more perfectly logical nnd critical than the earlier. It is not to be forgotten that Darwin was engaged in a controversy. The "Origin of Species" was not merely a study of the causes and history of organic evolution, but an argument to uphold the theory of evolution against that of the immutability of organic forms. It was written to convince a public which the author well knew to hold deep-rooted prejudices against his conclusions, and in his feeling of triumph at posssessing an argument based on what seemed the undeniable effects of human selection, he was led to lay too much stress on the analogous process in nature, and sometimes did not see clearly the limitations of that process. The error has been reproduced in intensified form in the works of some of Darwin's disciples. Now that the controversy has been fought out, biologists are beginning to study more calmly and more successfully the processes of organic modification, instead of merely proclaiming the perfections of the Darwinian system.

Allusion was made above to the anthropomorphic character of Darwin's central conception, and a comparison naturally suggests itself between that conception, and other anthropomorphic views of the universe which have prevailed at successive periods of human history. The earliest and crudest philosophy considers all the conspicuous objects in nature as beings with passions, desires, and wills similar to those of a man, and inquires no further into the origin of these objects. Eventually this stage of thought is replaced by the idea of one supreme Being with vast powers, but still essentially human in character, who created all things out of nothing very much in the condition in which they exist. This idea has been more persistent with regard to living beings than with regard to the not living. The evolution of the solar system from a nebula, and of the earth in its present condition from a red-hot mass, was generally admitted long before the evolution of the organic world. In place of the idea that species were originally created with their present structure and relations, Darwin set up the conception that by a process of selection in nature similar to that which man exercises on domesticated organisms, the existing complicated system of living beings has been evolved by gradual change from a much simpler original system. The Darwinian argument is not on a very different level from that of the argument from design. The teleologist like Darwin draws a parallel between the effects of human operations and the phenomena of nature. He points to a machine made by human ingenuity, such as a watch: in the watch, every part has its special purpose, which is subservient to the main end, that the hands shall move round the dial at a certain rate. Similarly, when we see the woodpecker with each organ subservient to the main purpose of the animal, to obtain its necessary food supply from insects beneath the bark of trees, we are to infer that some mind much more ingenious than that of man planned and constructed the organization of the woodpecker.

Darwin points to the instances in which man by selection has altered the organization of certain forms till they are more capable of serving his wants or pleasures, and infers that by the selection caused by the survival of the fittest, all organisms have been gradually modified until they have attained their present marvellously perfect adaptation to the conditions under which they live. But our comprehension of the evolution of organic forms will not be complete until it is a constituent part of the conception of universal evolution. That conception itself may be said in one sense to be anthropomorphic if it is found when completely analysed to rest upon a belief in the persistence of force which is derived from our own consciousness of muscular effort. But this is a general and philosophical anthropomorphism, while Darwin's is particular and empirical. When we have reached a real comprehension of organic evolution, we shall explain the modification of organisms by human cultivation as a particular instance of the general laws of modification and not *vice-versâ*. In an imperfect way we can do this even now. We can see clearly enough that the causes of modification and of inheritance are the same in cultivated as in wild organisms. We can see that the selection of certain individuals by man is, objectively considered, the survival of those individuals which are best adapted to the conditions of life, some of those conditions being human needs and desires.

But before we can attain a complete conception of universal evolution we must discover how to fill up, at least in thought, the chasm between the living and the not living.

The question of the origin of life, the genesis of the first living beings, was never discussed by Darwin. In his first work he did not even allude to the inference from his arguments that man must have descended from some lower form of mammal, and be related by community of descent with the apes, although the inference was immediately made by those who read his work, vehemently combated by some, and as emphatically supported by others. All that Darwin says, is:—

"There is grandeur in this view of life, with its several powers, having been originally breathed by the Creator into a few forms or into one; and that whilst this planet has gone on cycling according to the fixed law of gravity, from so simple a beginning endless forms most beautiful and most wonderful have been, and are being, evolved."

But as Darwin's spirit of inquiry and speculation could not be stopped by the dogma that species were created at the beginning as they now exist, so subsequent thinkers have speculated as to the origin of the primordial forms of life, notwithstanding that their leader was content to account for the first organisms by the power of the Creator. And here we have a curious anomaly. In other classes of phenomena, and in the transmutation of species, we can point to processes actually going on in the present condition of things as similar to the processes which must have caused the changes of which we find records in former periods of the earth's evolution. Marine fossils of former epochs are now found on hill-tops, and beaches are actually being raised by gradual elevation at the present day above the level of the sea. The phenomena of the glacial period can be illustrated by the effects of the glaciers of Switzerland; the formation of coal can be compared to the modern accumulation of peat, and the origin of many species from one can be seen to be actually going on in the formation of several domestic breeds of pigeons from one. It is thus very tempting to conclude that if living organisms were once formed from unorganized matter, the same process ought to be going on now. And this conclusion has been drawn by more than one writer. Mr. G. H. Lewes, for example, writes:—

"I cannot see the evidence which would warrant the belief that Life originated solely in one microscopic lump of protoplasm on one single point of our earth's surface; on the contrary, it is more probable that from innumerable and separate points of this teeming earth myriads of protoplasts sprang into existence, whenever and wherever the conditions of the formation of organized substance were present. It is probable that this has been incessantly going on, and that every day new protoplasts appear, struggle for existence, and serve as food for more highly organized rivals; but whether an evolution of the lower forms is or is not still going on, there can be no reluctance on the part of every believer in evolution to admit that when organized substance was first evolved, it was evolved at many points."

Unfortunately for the "probability," every attempt to discover an exception to the general rule *omne vivum e vivo* has hitherto absolutely failed, and it is curious that Lewes should so confidently argue about the probability of the recent origin of organisms from inorganic matter without referring to the celebrated controversy on "spontaneous generation." Up to the present time we have absolutely no analogy to guide us in forming a conception of the origin of living things from inorganic matter, and we have no more reason, scientifically speaking, to talk of the origin of life than of the origin of matter or of energy, however fascinating speculation may be on either point. It is interesting that at first sight it would seem necessary that the first organisms which lived on this planet must have been plants in the physiological sense, must have been able to obtain the energy necessary for their existence by acting on the rays of the sun, and so separating carbon from carbonic acid and forming compounds containing stored potential energy. But this can only be done in the presence of chlorophyll, and a unit of protoplasm possessing chlorophyll is more complex than one without chlorophyll. To get over the difficulty of the earliest living thing on this view, not being the simplest possible, Professor Lankester suggests that the first evolved forms were animals, and were produced only after a long process of evolution of carbon compounds, which produced first not living albuminoids and then living protoplasm which, in the first period of its life, fed on the antecedent stages of its own evolution. But at present we cannot form any conception of the process by which the first living beings could be evolved. Organic compounds have been produced by synthesis, and it is possible that in the surroundings where life first began albuminoids may have been produced from combinations of the elements. But no synthesis has ever produced living protoplasm, which was able to continue its life by feeding, and reproduce its kind by sub-division or gemmation. The protoplasm of the protozoan, which exhibits no other reproduction but total division, is immortal, although the ultimate elements of which it is composed are continually giving place to others. In compound organisms, although the individual dies, it is derived from a cell which has had through the ages a continuous life of whose beginning we can form no idea. The philosopher who attempts to trace the evolution of the solar system downwards from a diffused nebula, and the naturalist who traces back the history of organic evolution to the simplest forms of living beings, are both finally stopped by the impenetrable mystery of the origin of life. We can form no hypothesis of the beginning of life because we have at present reached no ultimate comprehension of the nature of living processes.

> "Flower in the crannied wall,
> I pluck you out of the crannies,
> Hold you here, root and all in my hand.
> Little flower—but if I could understand
> What you are, root and all, and all in all,
> I should know what God and man is."

J. T. CUNNINGHAM.

VI.

DANTE GABRIEL ROSSETTI

POET AND PAINTER

THE following Essay is the work—the most mature *literary* work—of the late Peter Walker Nicholson, Artist, whose sad and sudden death in the autumn of last year deprived Scottish art of one of its most promising votaries, and cut short a career fraught with sanguine interest to all who watched it. Mr. Nicholson took a warm interest in this Series, as is witnessed by his contribution of the happy and graceful design for the cover, and had promised to revise the present Essay with a view to its appearing therein. This, unfortunately, he had not accomplished, and the Essay came into the editor's possession pretty much as it was originally read before the Dialectic Society of the University of Edinburgh. With the exception, then, of the alterations absolutely necessary when an address to an audience is changed to an essay for readers, the original MS. has not been departed from. It will be only just, then, that the reader should bear in mind that the Essay lacks those finishing touches which the maturer judgment and skill of the author would certainly have bestowed upon it.

DANTE GABRIEL ROSSETTI.

FIFTY years ago there was a decided reaction towards mediævalism. In England it affected religion ; on the Continent it affected art. The pale nerveless works which crowd German galleries were mostly the outcome of this renaissance. Cornelius and Overbeck were the chief factors in beginning, as their pictures are very powerful reasons for ending, the German phase of this movement. In England, however, it bore splendid fruit. The Oxford movement in religion, either directly or indirectly, turned men's minds to the stagnant state of affairs generally. The time was ripe for a new departure in art. In poetry the old traditions had been swept away long before by Burns, later by Scott, Wordsworth, Byron, Coleridge, Shelley, and Keats. Tennyson, Browning, and Mrs. Browning, Arnold, and Clough were the voices which one by one broke into song. But art was still imprisoned. Turner, it is true, had done work for all men and for all time. He had painted the labour and sorrow and the passing away of men. But his work was too phenomenal, too individual ever to found a school sufficiently broad to reform art in all its various fields.

His work was too often misunderstood, or too often admired on account of the very qualities in it least worthy of praise. His work was too elemental, too absolute in its dominant qualities ever to cease being individual. So art still continued bound in spite of Turner's divine subtlety of changing light and wandering shade, of up-soaring splendour of the moon, of calm quiet beauty of noonday, of supreme gleam of crimson and glowing sunlight gold, of fading mists and tremulous sweetness of clouds, of dim mountain distances and far withdrawn glories of tumultuous sun-kissed seas. Ruskin wrote the first and second parts of "Modern Painters," reducing to science the wayward and instinctive works of Turner. But the end was not yet. Art was more hopelessly commonplace than before. The great style of Gainsborough, of Reynolds, had been vulgarised by the successive efforts of Copley, West, and Lawrence, and to a still greater extent by their followers. Based chiefly on the work of Constable and Bonnington, a new art was rising in France. As yet it was not recognised. Millet and Corot, Daubigny and Rousseau, were making a stand against the so-called Heroic School, as in literature, years before, a similar stand, or rather a very decided onslaught, had been made by Victor Hugo and Theophile Gautier against the stilted classicism of the Academy.

In England there duly arose the now famous Pre-Raffaelite Brotherhood. The more I examine their work the more clearly I am of the opinion that the whole movement originated with Dante Gabriel Rossetti, partly because the early work of all these men was very much of a similar nature—a similarity which has ceased as each painter found his individuality, while the characteristics of the early work of Rossetti continued to be present in all his work done afterwards. And this quality which we now recognise as distinctively his, was in the earlier days of the Brotherhood common to them all. This feeling was so strange, so utterly removed from any other phase of contemporary artistic thought as at once to attract attention. It is scarcely necessary to say that it also attracted ridicule. This ridicule seems requisite for the existence of any new movement. It is what Carlyle would call its "baphometic fire-baptism." This so-called Pre-Raffaelite Brotherhood proved its vitality by surviving this very torrent of baptismal abuse.

<u>Briefly and broadly the aim of this scheme was</u> to return to nature from the pedantic style of the Heroic School, with their lofty ideas as to the unfitness of ordinary truth, with their so-called Raffaelesque grace and Raffaelesque nobility, which required backgrounds of Palladian architecture and trailing drapery before all other things;—who called it needful in the case of one figure being dark against light, that another should be light against dark, that the hands of one should be up and the hands of another down, and various other stringently requisite duties of opposition, with the single exception perhaps that utter inanity of expression in one countenance was not regarded as a sufficient reason for any differing expression in any other. These good people went their way mightily pleased with their improvements, their balancing, their triangular, their circular, their elliptical compositions, with their improved scheme so far in advance of uncomposing, unbalancing nature, who, *tant pis pour elle*, had not invented renaissance architecture, nor renaissance juxtapositions of dark and light, nor renaissance garments in the days of the apostles and prophets and evangelists, whose stately posings and vague grandiose gesticulations these painters dreamed of.

This was the attitude of the later Pre-Raffaelites. This, to paint things as they were, or, in the case of historical work, as they might reasonably be imagined to have happened, not as they might be fancied grandly or nobly to have happened. It was more than a mere technical revolution : it was the infusion into art of a new soul. In the work of Rossetti, with whom I more particularly deal at this time, there was a force of imagination, a present beauty subtle, sweet, benign, a quiet mystical, spiritual loveliness unknown to art since the days of Fra Angelico and Botticelli. The very soul of Mediævalism was in these monks,— that high, pure, intense consciousness of infinite existence, of which this life is but a momentary manifestation, in a realm filled with angels and the souls of men and women. In his picture of Mary's girlhood, the angel with long crimson wings, flamelike and radiant, is as real as the Virgin embroidering the lily, as St. Anna with her quiet patient look, as St. Joachim trimming the vines in the dim, sunny garden without. I, for one, feel beyond all question that the painter of this and of the Annunciation saw and felt the presence and reality of the one as clearly as of the others. Further, that this was to him no mere myth, no mere beautiful story, but what was long ago in Galilee. The Annunciation with its utter simplicity : the awakened girl with a faint look of expectation in her eyes, as she gazes at the angel beneath whose feet are flames, bearing a lily, again seems to me to give this feeling of reality. To the Virgin the angel is no strange unknown presence ; she has no fear, only a subtle expectation, a half-dazed wonder as one awakened from sleep. It seems to me that this picture is more essentially truthful, more expressive of reality than any others I have seen. We feel that the Virgin (as he wrote in his sonnet) was

> An angel-watered lily that near God
> Grows and is quiet.

We feel the whole force of that simple uneventful life in the little Jewish village, with its calm sequence of dawn; its clear hushed day-time filled with small household duties and homely hopes and fears; the twilight with its period of dreamy rest, as the deep rich luminous sky stretches beyond the little leaves of the fruit trees in the orchard; the hushed night filled with the tender music of whispering winds; the stealing shadows in the moonlit room, the noiseless ministry of angels, the companionship of peasant folk, the yearly return of the Passover; all the gentle pensive inevitable course of life of those to whom now turns the prophetic soul of this great world dreaming of things to come.

I do not wonder that Rossetti never showed his pictures in public. Among the work of an ordinary gallery his would be out of place, as those old French Lives of the Saints, with their delicate initials and quaint, beautiful illuminations with their childlike faith, would be out of place beside the turbulence of Victor Hugo, the polite sneer of Voltaire, the *soi-disant* "*naturalisme*" of M. Emile Zola. Rossetti's genius was of a nature alien from this age. To the British public, mediævalism seems rather an absurd theory. Its highest, holiest, aspirations seem at this time thin and trivial. It was this feeling that kept Rossetti from courting the public criticism. It was not as many suppose, an inferior knowledge of technique. His colour was so pure, so gorgeous, so strong, that no picture of the present day could stand beside it. Turner no more effectively dimmed the Academy of his day than would Rossetti have dimmed the Academy of ours.

Here it may probably be most fitting that I should say some words on the nature of Rossetti's work before beginning a detailed notice of his poetry and painting.

It is my feeling that Rossetti had a fixed standpoint from which he looked at life; that he did not change this;—that his painting was not the expression of one phase, nor his poetry the expression of another phase; but that he recorded his single perception in two ways. So his poetry sometimes seems to bring the colour, the force, the realization of painting; his pictures have the subtilty, the symbolism, the expression in some degree peculiar to verse.

It is not an easy task to determine the place of Rossetti among poets and painters. To a certain extent his work is individual and unique;—he is of kin with those mediæval painters whose faint frescoes are quietly fading away in little Italian churches; he is of kin too with those unknown men who first formed the sweet, rough lines of the Border Ballads; with the latter, by virtue of his simple and direct way of looking at life, with the former by reason of his no less simple and direct manner of gazing beyond into a land of spirits of which this world is but the expression. But again, and as a secondary aspect of his genius, he had in him as counteractive (or rather I should say because) of these qualities, a very strong sense of bodily beauty. He felt the presence of the body so forcibly, because he was so keenly aware of the existence of the soul, because a beautiful form is artistically the sign of a beautiful soul, because the spirit cannot otherwise be seen by mortals. Pure and lofty deeds, a gracious and beautiful form, these are the means in which the invisible is made visible. Had Rossetti not been a painter by nature his poetry would have been vague, thin, visionary. For his mind was of so mystical a nature, that had he not been very strongly aware of the symbolical form of expression, his verses would doubtless have been very intangible. For my own part, I feel that, in order to keep the balance at all, it was needful that he should have a more than usually powerful sense of outer existence. The result is a strange quality, reminding one in painting of the work of Leonardo da Vinci. Like the Italian master, the chief charm of his pictures is in the expression of feature. But there is now and again a more splendid and majestic beauty than is usually to be found in the work of the painter of Mona Lisa. The art of Giorgione is suggested by the broad rich masses of colour, now clear and luminous, now gleaming in sombre and sacred fitness of chord, by the stately repose of his men and women, whose calm of body and soul seem one with the dimly stealing light of quiet twilight hours. For them the tumult of life has passed away; its din has become hushed, whatever of sin and sorrow, of joy and sweetness has been theirs, exists now only as a memory.

Side by side with those qualities, and to some extent because of them, are these other characteristics very noteworthy in his verse, of great tragic power, of large grasp of the essential features of life. The very breadth of his view of these things tends to disable his force in this field. His knowledge, or rather, perhaps, his feeling, was not sufficiently minute to give mastery of character—he is subtile, but it is subtilty of symbolism and thought and emotion rather than subtilty of circumstance and action for which he looks.

At the age of seventeen Rossetti wrote his poem, "The Blessed Damozel." It is hard to find words fitly to express the emotions touched by these verses. Higher and purer and sweeter than any words in this English tongue, they gently bear the listener beyond this earth into a calm and sacred air, yet not beyond all changes of pure human hope and fear, and high and holy love. In this poem, and these two, "The Portrait" and "The Stream's Secret," are drawn the two sides of a lasting love, a love that outlives death and change. The poems seem to me to be, with the sonnets, the most individual work Rossetti has done. There is a touch of Dante in them; but to modern men there is little likeness. Indeed, the only man in present day literature (except, of course, those who are avowedly his pupils), the only man who has the same sort of qualities as Rossetti, is Cardinal J. H. Newman. Newman represents the dogmatic and logical side of mediævalism as Rossetti represents the mystical side. Both look beyond the shows of the world; each passes somewhat into the special field of the other. I doubt if my meaning will be plain except to those who have studied carefully the "Hymn" and the "Dream of Gerontius." There is in both men a simple, direct, almost childlike way of looking at death. It is the passing into another place; but the younger poet, unlike the elder, could not fancy any severing of the eternal love begun on earth. The feeling of his poem, "The Blessed Damozel," is essentially mediæval. The mediæval intellect was to a very notable extent realistic. It dealt with things and symbols, not Hegelian abstractions. It was artistic, pictorial. Hence the "Blessed Damozel" is no dim far away spirit, but is subtly imagined as really living in heaven. The lover on earth cannot in his dreams separate her body from her soul. The one is the counterpart of the other. So the poem is filled with fine human touches. These are of infinite artistic value. The supernatural or spiritual is only of magical and passionate interest when it touches the borderland of mortal life; it is then to us a spiritualized humanity rather than a mysterious presence from an infinitely distant land. In the "Blessed Damozel" such touches are sparingly given, but always with unerring instinct. This insistance on the spiritual side of life is the dominant note of all his poetry. In the "Blessed Damozel" we can see how little difference he felt between life and love on earth and in the highest heaven. In the portrait we see how the lover remaining on earth makes his dead lady a centre for all thoughts and works till he should wake from the decay of life.

> "Even so, where heaven holds breath and hears
>   The beating heart of love's own breast,
> Where round the secret of all spheres
>   All angels lay their wings to rest.
> How shall my soul stand rapt and awed,
> When, by the new birth borne abroad
>   Throughout the music of the suns,
>   It enters in her soul at once,
> And knows the silence there for God!

> "Here with her face doth Memory sit
>   Meanwhile, and wait the day's decline,
> Till other eyes shall look from it,
>   Eyes of the Spirit's Palestine.
> Even than the old gaze tenderer;
> While hopes and aims long lost with her
>   Stand round her image side by side,
>   Like tombs of pilgrims that have died
> About the holy sepulchre."

In the sonnets he tells us that all sin as all good is lasting, that not only his lost love will meet him in the golden heavens, but how each lost day, each base action, will crowd around him with cold commemorative eye, saying :—

> "I am thyself, and I, and I,
> And those thyself to all eternity."

For absolute sin is not so hideous in this man's sight as these virtues which are vain, which bear no fruit, which droop and die; these are the sorriest things that enter hell. To him a real love is so pure, so noble, so holy, that he can imagine no change in it through all the æons of eternal heavenly life. But this belief did not, as it never will, keep back the feeling of utter loneliness and forlorn sorrow, the knowledge that the light of life has for a space fled away, the dreamy wandering in a twilight world, the awestruck, patient waiting, made luminous by a distant hope, that from out the sleep of the grave their souls should rise, through gleams as of watered light and dull drowned waifs of day to a more perfect life.

> "Those who walk in willow-wood
> With hollow faces burning white,"

weeping for the lost love on earth, which they shall regain, have visions of an after-time when the—

> "Wan soul in that golden air,
> Between the scriptured petals softly blown,
> Peers breathless for the gift of grace unknown.

> "Ah, let none other written spell soe'er,
> But only the one hope's one name be there,
> Not less nor more, but even that word alone."

If by any sad and desolate chance no future should be, where there is only left by death a fleeting memory of the past—

> "Oh love, my love, if I no more should see
> Thyself, nor on the earth the shadow of thee,
>   Nor image of thine eyes in any spring,—
> How then should sound upon Life's darkening slope
> The ground-whirl of the perished leaves of Hope,
>   The wind of Death's imperishable wing?"

Such a man could do no trivial work. To him all things appear, as to Spinoza, *sub specie eternitatis*. His every act he knew to live for ever,—his life on earth, his love on earth, to be but the beginning of a life and a love hereafter. The body to him was but a symbol, whose significance and preciousness lay in its being the tarrying place of the soul. Hence his work is of a great and grave character as befits the expression through all signs and symbols of the fair presences of which we and all we see are but the shadows. His paintings seem not so much transcripts of reality as of a dimly-seen translation, so to speak, of some far-off sound or colour well known, but too ethereal and too holy for mortal ears. For him the spirit world, "dumb to Homer, dumb to Keats, him even" had a voice, as it had to the returned soul of the dead man in the Platonic vision, who passed over the river of forgetfulness, but whose soul was not defiled.

"The best of art," says Ruskin, "are but shadows." Strange it may seem that this pale shadowy art of his, so fair, so subtle, so dim, should have a more real quality than those others whose work seems stronger and more lasting. His poems and pictures which seem most realistic are in reality the most symbolical. In his "House of Life" he tells us how small things are of great moment, and how great things are of none avail. In this spirit and with this view of life was the "Blessed Damozel" written. As a work of art, it reaches a rare perfection; the touches of great, clear imagination, the charm of tenderly-chosen words, the superb refluence of music echoing between earth and heaven, as the Damozel speaks and her lover replies,—set this poem as peerless in English song. The force of imagination is shown in the touch telling how, as she leaned over the golden bar, the souls mounting up to God went by her like thin flames; how the bar on which she leant grew warm; how the old prayers granted, melt like a little cloud; or how the five handmaidens of the Lady Mary fashion birth-robes for those just born, being dead. The close of the poem is very quiet, a calm so great that (as the old dramatist says) "one might hear all the angels singing out of heaven."

> "I wish that he were come to me,
> For he will come," she said.
> "Have I not prayed in heaven? on earth,
> Lord, Lord, hath he not prayed?"

For clear perfection of music, a melody more involved in its richness than that of the "Blessed Damozel," turn to "Love's Nocturne." Verse after verse, line after line, is filled with the glory of golden words, suffused by the dim air of dreamland. This poem is a good example of his mystical vision. The man in dreamland meeting his own soul, and sending it from thence to his lady, is a counterpart of a strange drawing, where he shows two mortals met by their ghosts. We can fancy the spirits to belong to the future life of the youth and maiden, upbraiding them for the past. Like the Lost Days they rise each on a murdered self with awful presence. I have already referred to "The Stream's Secret" and "The Portrait." In the former poem he considers the stream as a symbol of the love first born by its banks. Very noticeable here are the fine references to landscape, to wit, the subtle touch of the invisible burthen of the "sun grown cold," and "the moon's labouring gaze," the lines indicating the rush of the stream in flood-time, the water lapping in the cave. In "The Portrait" is the fine simile of how these memories of old days are disavowed by day, and nought is left to see or hear.

> " Only in solemn whispers now,
> At night-time these things reach mine ear;
> When the leafy shadows at a breath
> Shrink in the road, and all the heath,
> Forest, and water, far and wide,
> In linkèd starlight glorified,
> Lie like the mystery of death."

"The Last Confession" is the poem in his first volume most like the "Rose Mary" and "King's Tragedy" in his second. Here he touches a realistic objective story, though he still keeps his subjective manner of thought. For it is noteworthy that in this poem the causes of the crime are entirely symbolical: the episode of the laugh, repeated by the child, could only be imagined by one of Rossetti's subtle way of thought; the little incident of the Cupid, the dream of God blessing the world,—the whole texture of the poem is made up of symbols. The involutions, the inversion of time, the hesitancy, the clear memory of little things, the burning, searing picture of the day of death, remind one somewhat of Browning's supreme studies; remind one of some portions of the " Ring and the Book." But this poem is different from the work of the elder poet. It is clearer,—I had almost said subtler. It is more monochromatic in its intensity than is Browning's usual work. At one point it touches one of those heights of tragic force reached in this century only by two men—Victor Hugo and Browning—when the confessing man tells the father to make certain of his meaning, lest by any chance, misunderstanding him, he give absolution :—

> "If you mistake my words,
> And so absolve me, Father, the great sin
> Is yours, not mine: mark this, your soul shall burn
> With mine for it."

The remark following as to the "Latin shriekings" is alike of that high order of daring imagination. The more I read this poem, the more I am impressed by its enormous power. I rank it with the very finest work of Browning. Better it cannot be, and higher praise I cannot give.

Of Dante at Verona, time will not permit me to speak at length. It is a quiet, restrained piece of art, condensed and reticent to a quite marvellous extent, filled with picturesque lines as where he tells of how the lords of Florence saw the proscripts kneel in the dust on the shrine steps. Or again the lines telling of the life at the court of Can Grande.

This poem is a fine appendix to some of his pictures. The lines, telling how he met Beatrice in Florence, and again in Paradise, call to mind the noble colour and beautiful grace of the designs showing the earthly and the heavenly meetings. The last in the calm of Paradise, when the lady says, "Even I, even I am Beatrice."

"The Burden of Nineveh" is a very strong poem,

with a wide view of history, suggested by the sight of an Assyrian bull being borne into the British Museum. At some future time, he dreams, when London is in ruins, antiquarians may conclude from finding this sculptured beast that this was the manner of god we worshipped. The fate of Nineveh, with its pride and pomp, suggests the fate of other cities, when with sense half shut,—

> " He sees the crowd of kerb and rut
>   Go past as marshalled to the street,
> Of ranks in gypsum quaintly cut,
>   It seemed in one same pageantry.
> They followed forms which had been erst:
>   So hap, till on my sight should burst
> That future of the best or worst,
>   When some may question which was first,
> Of London or of Nineveh."

And the bull seems a fit type of our modern life with its weight of superstition and care.

There is one verse to my mind as great an example of strong imagination as any other I ever read, and is always associated in my mind as an artistic triumph with the great burst of poetry at the end of Carlyle's description of the taking of the Bastille. The reference is of course to the temptation of Christ:—

> " The day when he Pride's lord and Man's
>   Showed all the kingdoms at a glance.
> To Him, before whose countenance
>   The years recede, the years advance,
> And said, ' Fall down and worship me.'
>   'Mid all the pomp beneath that look,
> Then stirrred there haply some rebuke,
>   When to the winds the Lost Pools shook,
> And in those tracts, of life forsook,
>   That knew thee not, O Nineveh."

One who so sees facts, necessarily has that gift of proportion of relation, which is present in all great art, and without which no tragic power is possible, which enables one truly to estimate this life and all its changes. To see beyond the appearance, the manifestation, to the great unity of purpose underlying all things, is to see with clear vision the infinite course of human progress beyond the pathos of broken human hearts, the tragedy of thwarted human endeavour. It is to see the relative and half truth widely in the light of the absolute truth. It is (again to use the phrase of Spinoza) to see the world *sub specie eternitatis.*

This attitude applies to the next poem I mention— "Jenny."

The motto prefixed to the poem showed that Rossetti was well aware how it might be received. But I do not think he was prepared to endure such calumny and misrepresentation as fell to his lot. The earliest and most virulent of his critics not long ago expressed great surprise that he could ever have so misunderstood the meaning of Rossetti's work. So it is, I fancy, with many others. One constantly meets with people who talk of this poem as a very choice selection of evil. Again I ask, do you imagine that the great and grave genius, who wrote "The Blessed Damozel," who wrote the sonnets "My Sister's Sleep," "The Card Player," "The Burden of Nineveh," "Dante at Verona;" who painted "The Girlhood of the Virgin," "The Annunciation," "The Passover in the Holy Family," "The Virgin in the House of John," the whole sequence of pictures relative to the Vita Nuova of Dante,—do you fancy he could do any ribald or trivial thing? I do not.

Of all work done in these days I know of none more pure, more intensely spiritual, more utterly removed from any evil than that of Dante Gabriel Rossetti, nor do I know of any poem which, when fully and closely understood, is more beautiful and sacred in its lofty purity than "Jenny." Indeed to it belongs the further merit of a triumphantly pure handling of a difficult subject.

Such themes may indeed be, nay, often are, evil; but in the hands of a great poet, never. By his very birthright he can utter nothing base. The poem "Jenny" is the frank recognition of a fact in life, but it is put in its proper light. No artist of any breadth can ignore such facts; but there are, unfortunately, people who can see very little else. Some of you may have noticed that Browning and Swinburne very often treat of the same subjects. But while Swinburne deals with a single emotion, Browning ranges afar, tracing from the first beginning, and following to the eventual end the workings of the passion. This largeness of thought, this keenness of vision,—this makes the elder poet's work of vast ethical import. It is the element in all dramatic writing, which in its absence makes littleness, and with its presence makes greatness. So in "Jenny," Rossetti traces the growth of the girl through life from the old days of childhood that seem to be—

> "Much older than any history
> That is written in any book,
> When she would lie in fields and look
> Along the ground through the blown grass,
> And wonder where the city was
> Far out of sight, whose brawl and bale
> They had told her even for a child's tale."

From this to the present, terrible reality, looking forward to the yet more awful future, he sees the entire life, he traces the causes, he compares, he weighs, he knows with subtle sympathy the fairer features, not wholly obscured; the dim possibility of goodness not wholly passed away, the pity of it, the dumb anguish that looks beneath it all, its true relation to the infinite sorrow of this world.

But for largeness of style, for beauty and force of thought, for sweetness and directness of wording, for height and depth of passion, for steady continuous flow and development of motion, for the full expression of all his various qualities of lyrical and dramatic power, the first place among his work is beyond all dispute held by the "Rose Mary." No such poem has been written since the "Ancient Mariner" and "Christabel" of Coleridge. It has the richness of these poems. It has their strange mingling of reality and romance, their resonance and their rare perfection of finish. Into the bare stern land of Northern Legend, that land so often made splendid by heroic deeds and made sacred by song, where every glen and hillside has its weird tale of love or of death, he has brought another element—the talisman, the beryl stone, with its dim, cloudy companionship of Eastern suggestiveness, with its reminiscent touches of the clash of arms in far lands and in olden days, when crusader and Turk met in deadly fight, of strange, remote places, "where swart Paynims pray." From these gathered threads of glowing Eastern and weird Northern romance, he has woven a majestic poem. It deals with the tragic things of existence, with all its moods of clear and tender and sweet beauty, with all its dark, terrible sorrow, with its mysteries of love and of death, with its passionate, fiery emotions of anger and hate, its infinite, inevitable burden of fallen and faded human lives. These touches telling how Rose Mary read the vision in the beryl-stone, how her heart fell as she knew that the future could only be seen by the pure, her complex, wandering thoughts as she beheld the lying pictures, the taking them for truth, the doom of the false lover, the marvellous beauty of these verses telling how the Rose Mary fancies her mother knew of her guilt, the force of the lines telling how the sin of Rose Mary became known to her mother.

> "Closely locked they cling without speech,
> And the mirrored souls shook each to each,
> As the cloud-moon and the water-moon
> Shake face to face when the dim stars swoon,
> In stormy bowers of the night's mid-noon."

The stormy tragic directness of the lines when she tells her of the slain man, the terrible pitiful loveliness of these others, sacred and splendid and sad with their swift keen simplicity, when the mother finds the message on the dead man's breast, how the face, late so fair, became very hateful, being now known, her bitter taunt as she throws down the lock of golden hair, the wealth of perfect words in the passage where Rose Mary strikes and breaks the beryl-stone, the faint, serene echoes of heavenly speech, falling like the blessing of the dew, fitly and fairly crowning the whole with their perfect music; these things, I say, place this poem on the very highest level of romantic art.

By this poem, as by no other, is Rossetti's claim of mastery made certain. And this claim is made more firm and lasting by the "King's Tragedy" and "The White Ship." These last works are very simple and direct. In the whole range of romantic poetry no clearer vision has been made known to us than the picture in the "Rose Mary" of the mother hurrying down the winding stair and getting swift glimpses of the hillside and woodland and stream through the narrow windows, or in the "King's Tragedy," of the woman meeting James by the Scottish sea, or in the hush of night in Perth.

> " Last night at mid-watch, by Aberdour,
>   When the moon was dead in the skies,
> O king, in a death-light of thine own
>   I saw thy shape arise.
>
> And in full season, as erst I said,
>   The doom had gained its growth ;
> And the shroud had risen above the neck
>   And covered thine eyes and mouth.
>
> And no moon woke, but the pale dawn broke,
>   And still thy soul stood there ;
> And I thought its silence cried to my soul
>   As the first rays crowned its hair.
>
> Since then have I journeyed fast and fain
>   In very despite of fate,
> Lest hope might still be found in God's will ;
>   But they drove me from thy gate.
>
> For every man on God's ground, O king,
>   His death grows up from his birth
> In a shadow plant perpetually;
>   And thine towers high, a black yew tree,
>   O'er the charterhouse of Perth !"

Such touches as these give the world assurance of a great poet. For such an one is measured, not by his execution, not by his felicity or suavity of touch, but by his breadth of human sympathy, by his knowledge of human passion.

We have heard it claimed for Rossetti that his work must be measured by special critical rules, that it is not like other work. I do not feel this. I hold that whatever in him cannot be widely understood is of little moment in his poetry or painting. I appeal to the catholic criticism, which understands his masters, Shakespeare and Dante. I appeal from the fashion that praises, as from the folly that blames, from the affectation of esoteric comprehension, on the one hand, as from the affectation of fastidious puritanism on the other. I appeal to the force and fervour, to the passion and pity of "Jenny," to the severe beauty, to the whole spiritual meaning of the sonnets, with their large view of life and love and death, to the sweet and sacred perfection of "The Blessed Damozel" and "My Sister's Sleep," to the high and clear light of "Ave" and "Staff and Scrip," to the rich and splendid music of "Love's Nocturne" and the "Stream's Secret," to the strength and significance of "The Burden of Nineveh" and "Dante at Verona," to the changing emotions and weird weaving of love and hate, of despair and hope, of things human and devilish and divine in the "Rose Mary" to the great and grave force of the "King's Tragedy" and the "White Ship," I appeal to these qualities in these poems as I appeal to the power and pathos and passion of all great singers; the criticism which is broad enough for these last is broad enough for Rossetti too. If special criticism be needed for any one it is assuredly for those who crawl beneath the board to pick up the scraps from the feast of their betters. For the thousand and one small piping rhymsters, who affect the manner of speech of all great men, for the whole tribe of parodists and plagiarists, a newer and other criticism is necessary, a criticism so broad as to include all inanity and feebleness whatever. Nor is this cry unknown with reference to his pictures. Again I appeal to "The Girlhood of the Virgin," to the "Annunciation," to "Found," to the sombre and nobly subdued colour of the " Dream of Dante," the majesty and repose of the " Blessed Damozel," the triumphant force and superb splendour and glory of " Fiametta," the beauty and dim inner gaze of " Memory," the perfect and ordered harmony of " Silence," the power and majesty of " How they met Themselves," the strange legendary feeling of the design " Michael Scott's Weaving," the brilliance and breadth of the " Blue Bower," the rich suffused depth of twilight tone in " The Virgin at the house of John," the mediæval directness of imagination and mastery of clear colour and delicate design of character and expression in the " St George." What vitality is in these works is precisely the vitality present in the work of Titian, of Giorgione, of Leonardo da Vinci, of Fra Angelico,—his nearest kin on art's side ;—precisely these qualities, on whose various degrees of presence we judge to be greater or less, the works of Velasquez and Rembrandt, of Turner, of Millet, of Michael Angelo.

In the space there is left at my disposal I can only refer briefly to his shorter poems, to his translations and his sonnets on pictures. Two poems, however, I should like to mention as being, to my mind, especially beautiful, the " Cloud Confines" and " Sunset Wings." I quote the latter of these, for its beautiful record of nature, its true mingling of painter's and poet's vision. You may with justice regard this as a connecting link between his song and art, although very many other poems stand in the same central place.

> " To-night this sunset spreads two golden wings,
>   Cleaving the western sky ;
> Winged too with wind it is, and winnowings
>   Of birds ; as if the day's last hour in rings
>   Of strenuous flight must die.

Sun-steeped in fire, the homeward pinions away
    Above the dovecot tops;
And clouds of starlings, ere they rest with day,
Sink, clamorous like mill-waters, at wild play,
    By turns in every copse.

Each tree heart-deep the wrangling rout receives,
    Save for the whirr within,
You could not tell the starlings from the leaves;
Then one great puff of wings, and the swarm heaves
    Away with all its din.

Ever thus hope's hours, in ever-eddying flight,
    To many a refuge tend;
With the first light she laughed, and the last light
Glows round her still; who, natheless in the night,
    At length must make an end.

And now the mustering rooks innumerable
    Together sail and soar,
While for the day's death, like a tolling knell,
Unto the heart they seem to cry, Farewell,
    No more, farewell, no more!

Is not hope plumed, as 'twere a fiery dart?
    And oh! thou dying day,
Even as thou goest, must she too depart,
And sorrow fold such pinions on the heart
    As will not fly away?"

It seems to me that Rossetti did not express himself in painting with that fulness and force so characteristic of the sister art. But to some extent his poetry and painting, leaving the fields peculiar to each, seem to meet in a land midway between, and we see as it were painted poems and written pictures; a borderland, in a figure, of our life, whence we have great glimpses into the quiet places of souls outside our being. His expression of this is twofold, each single expression inadequate, but both explanatory, and in great measure clearly, not like Blake, vaguely visionary, but as

Plato and Dante, following the path of life into the arcana of pure being. On this borderland he has wandered, and his pictures, with their mystic symbols and strange mingling of body and soul, give partial expression to his visions. In his picture of Michael Scott's wooing there are dim forms bending over and looking in from the outer world. In the Sonnets he has pictured such pale, wistful faces gazing into our life, old memories, ghosts of lost days and sinful things, sweet and sorrowful eyes of those who walk in willowwood. These are again shown in that marvellous sequence of pictures, which holds a position in his painting analogous to that held in his poetry by his sonnets. Let us consider these. Rossetti's art, let us frankly recognise, was one-sided. True, it was the nobler side of things he saw, but to him much of the outer world was as a dream. In his later work there is to some extent a greater breadth of grasp, a greater feeling for the pathos of human life, but also a growing mysticism. There is, in all the series of heads to which I have referred, a certain vagueness of emotion, as of a dim remembrance of sorrow, some faint, half-heard echo of joy, some strange after-glow of a vanished love, all things are etherealised, seen calmly, quietly, in the dim vesper light of far-away days. They come to us as a new thing, but have, too, the keen, sweet quality of a half remembered music heard in swift momentary pulsations. They seem primal facts of our life, memory and purity and lost love, circled by all subtle, symbolical suggestions, as the strong, massive, weighty force of thought in his sonnets is surrounded by the flower-like beauty of gracious fancies.

This mental position was characteristic of mediæval

art. In the old Pre-Raffaelite work, and to a great extent in the work of Raffaelle, Michael Angelo, Titian, Giorgione, Leonardo da Vinci, passion and joy, all sorrowful and serene changes of life are seen in a retrospective vision. In Giorgione's great Venetian Pastoral in the Louvre, all nature seems a dream; the men and women are very calm and quiet in that hushed and golden air. The music even has ceased, but its thin, ethereal breath still lingers and wanders, mingled with the faint and tender touch of gently refluent water. But to such painters, as to all men, came sometimes the surge of a great passion, a strong consciousness that the world is too large to pass as a dream. Outside their dusky orchard close, with its twilight of rich, solemn, luminous colours, there is the infinite sorrow and the pain of finite souls that yearn. Rossetti felt this, but his art required that it should be expressed in a lower key, as an echo. He paints, no less than the great men of other ages, the dominant and the supreme moments of existence. The note of a whole life is struck in such pictures as "The Death of Lady Macbeth," "The Carlisle Towers," "The Hesterna Rosa," "The Return of Tibullus to Delia;" yet the emotion is purified, as it were; translated from the terror, the swift, fugitive pulse of passion, into the calm, pure region of beauty. The work deals not so much with the incidental outcome as the deep spiritual principles whence it springs. It is a retrospective vision. We hear the tale, we feel the emotion, as we feel it in Keats, while the nightingale sang in the woods under the throbbing purple of the summer night. There is no finer wording of this quality of emotion than in Rossetti's sonnet to the Madonna of the Rocks by Leonardo da Vinci. One who examines the picture and carefully reads the sonnet, gets a wonderful insight into Rossetti's individuality.

> "Mother, is this the darkness of the end,
> The shadow of death? and is that outer sea
> Infinite imminent eternity?
> And does the death-pang, by man's seed sustained
> In time's each instant, cause thy face to bend
> Its silent prayer upon the Son, while he
> Blesses the dead with his hand silently
> To his long day, which hours no more offend?
> Mother of Grace, the pass is difficult,
> Keen as these rocks, and the bewildered souls
> Throng it like echoes, blindly shuddering through;
> Thy name, O Lord, each spirit's voice extols,
> Whose pæan abides in the dark avenue
> Amid the bitterness of things occult."

There are two phases of the higher artistic emotion. Some men have no knowledge of life but as a dimly remote memory; it comes to them from far away, not otherwise than as one might behold forms in a mirror.

> "Deep in the gleaming glass
> She sees all past things pass,
> And all sweet life that was
> Lie down and die."

The work of Morris in the present day shows much of this quality.

The other way seems to me to be the manner of some of the greatest artists of all time. From the height of a great exaltation the speech of this world becomes thin and scarcely heard, all small and trivial things are silent, only the voices of humanity are heard any more. The accidental, the momentary fades away. In the loneliness of lofty thought a wider view of the life is gained, the artistic work is beautiful and very calm; there is in it that simplicity, that largeness we feel when we see a wide stretch of meadow land, of mountain, of forest, and broad gleams of water, united, glorified in the soft radiance of a golden afternoon. Rossetti stood midway between these.

In his little poem of St. Hilary he has shown how impossible it is for one to escape from this world. Into the land of clear colours and stories of his art enters the strange murmur of the outer humanity.

One afternoon, tired of work, I had been wandering through the Latin quarter of Paris. By chance, I crossed the bridge and found myself under the shadow of the fair Sainte Chapelle. Climbing a narrow stair I emerged from the din and the laughter, from the mire of the streets, into that dreamlike church, so sacred, so splendid, so rich with the most holy memories of old-time chivalry, with the sweetest and purest flowerage of old-time thought and art, with its infinite subtlety of radiant and luminous and gorgeous colours, with its streaming glories of jewelled light, its gracious tracery of perfect lines, its utter quiet and loneliness, filled and thrilled with the very peace of heaven, here, if at all, surely here, in this saintly shrine, should all the sound of earth be hushed. But after a little space I heard the dull strained sounds of the great life without rushing past, as flow terribly, foully, under bridge and quay, the waters of the dark stream. I left the chapel; a few steps and I had re-entered the city of Francois Villon, of Victor Hugo, and I saw the towers, so significant, of Notre Dame de Paris, under whose shadow, on summer afternoons, lies the Morgue.

In such a land of quiet beauty Rossetti dwelt, but not always. When touched into realism (as men call it) he used other means of expression. The glowing wrath of the sonnet on the "Refusal of Aid between Nations," that on "The Bastille," and that other on the "Survivors of Trafalgar," give evidence of different powers. But his instinct turned to the quiet repose of earliest art. The truly artistic mind is ever instinctive, it is not scientific; it is affected by feeling, it gains an impression. This impression may often be partial and even wrong, but it is the result of certain qualities in the object, being coincident with certain qualities in the mind of the artist. Truth is arrived at, not by analytic means, but by a synthetic method. It is proportioned by chance drifts of apprehension, by stray waifs of fact and of fancy. The after-work of moulding, purifying, and refining is almost of a quite objective character. It is, to some extent, mere artizan work. There is of course a necessary exercise of the very finest qualities of his nature, but the real artistic spirit is chiefly occupied with the prior and less tangible task of instinctive acquisition and assimilation. We see the character of a man in his work, because we feel he chooses certain effects above others: not by his technical powers, but by the same qualities of mind which influence his selection, is touched into life his method of expression. This the raiment; the body making present the shadowy intangible soul. It is of no use merely as a means of recording the fleeting impression. So soon as this becomes a compulsory exercise of research, of analysis, of critical inquisitiveness, it fades to a lower place. These things belong to impression entirely. This seems to me very chiefly a quality of Rossetti, as it is the quality of all the finest art. When one has grasped his idea, his beautiful, subtle expression is forgotten. It is in perfect sympathy with the soul of his art, now severe, grave, simple; now dainty, polished, clear, superb; now rich, shadowy, mysterious.

You know the story of the Lady of Shalott. She

saw all the world in a mirror till she became sick of shadows, and turned to the living, throbbing world itself. Rossetti's art is different. He turned from the world to the semblance; he saw a strange, radiant image, the primal truths, as one looking through a prism sees the colour of common objects reduced to their primitive tint, the grey of life changed into intensest rose and gold and heavenly blue.

It was the boast of Goodwin that he would write a book of such a nature that no one reading it could remain the same manner of man any longer. So it is with Rossetti's pictures. No one who ever has clearly felt his influence can lose it; for his view of the value and significance of life is widened, and a new hope for art is awakened. The art tendency of the present day is towards truth, and we may expect much crude effort toward that end. As a factor in raising the ideal, in showing that truth is more than a mere literal transcript of nature, that it is a subtle and holy thing, Rossetti's work will be of very great value. As a phase of art it is not my wish, as it is not in my power, to estimate its importance.

It may be that I have laid too great accentuation on the artistic side of Rossetti's nature. I have been, however, far from forgetting the ethical tendency of his work. This seems to me to be no insignificant feature of his genius: all the more so because it is in a great measure unconscious. He has not the direct force of religious or philosophical teaching so openly evident in the work of Browning, not the swift, strong insight which gives value to the critical quasi-pessimism of Arnold; not the agnostic hopelessness of Clough, nor the comparatively firm faith which informs with fervour and with light the verse of Mrs. Browning or of Tennyson; but he has that quality present in all their poetry; that sympathy, that pity for the foiled, circuitous wanderer, for the ever-eluded grasp of eager, human souls. This, to some extent the key-note of modern thought, finds expression in his poem, " Cloud Confines," not unmingled with the clear melody of a triumphant song.

> " The day is dark and the night
>   To him that would search their heart;
>   No lips of cloud that will part
> Nor morning song in the light:
>   Only, gazing alone,
>   To him wild shadows are shown,
>   Deep under deep unknown,
> And height above unknown height.
>   Still we say as we go,—
>   'Strange to think by the way,
>   Whatever there is to know,
>   That shall we know one day.'

> " The past is over and fled;
>   Named new, we name it the old;
>   Thereof some tale hath been told,
> But no word comes from the dead;
>   Whether at all they be,
>   Or whether as bond or free,
>   Or whether they too were we,
> Or by what spell they have sped.
>   Still we say as we go,—
>   'Strange to think by the way,
>   Whatever there is to know,
>   That shall we know one day.'

> " What of the heart of hate
>   That beats in thy breast, O time?
>   Red strife from the furthest prime,
> And anguish of fierce debate;
>   War that shatters her slain,
>   And peace that grinds them as grain,
>   And eyes fixed ever in vain
> On the pitiless eyes of fate.

>   Still we say as we go,—
>   'Strange to think by the way,
>   Whatever there is to know,
>   That shall we know one day.'
>
> "What of the heart of love
>   That bleeds in thy breast, O man?
>   Thy kisses snatched 'neath the ban
> Of fangs that mock them above;
>   Thy bells prolonged unto knells,
>   Thy hope that a breath dispels,
>   Thy bitter forlorn farewells,
> And the empty echoes thereof?
>   Still we say as we go,—
>   'Strange to think by the way,
>   Whatever there is to know,
>   That shall we know one day.'
>
> "The sky leans dumb on the sea,
>   Aweary with all its wings;
>   And oh! the song the sea sings
> Is dark everlastingly.
>   Our past is clean forgot,
>   Our present is and is not,
>   Our future's a sealed seedplot,
> And what betwixt them are we?
>   We who say as we go—
>   'Strange to think by the way,
>   Whatever there is to know,
>   That shall we know one day.'"

But although his last work, it is not his only expression of his ethical position. Here and there it is heard, in the tendency of most of his poems, chiefly and sufficiently in the marvellous spiritual introspection of the sonnets.

He has wrought as did the old Italian painter to whom appeared his own soul saying—" Take now thine art unto thee, and paint me thus, as I am, to know me; weak, as I am and in the weeds of this time; only with eyes which seek out labour, and with a faith not learned, yet jealous of prayer. Do this; so shall thy soul stand before thee always, and perplex thee no more."

Art done in this spirit must be lasting, for it touches eternal truths, and will have life when much of our present day work, dealing with the momentary and fleeting fashion of the hour, shall have passed into the darkness with fit companionship of tongues that have ceased and of knowledge that has vanished away.

And again, further, when we think how much of his influence is found in the beauty and force and delicate finish of Morris, in the strength and lyric speed and perfect, plastic, verbal power of Swinburne, in the calm, pure design and clear, sweet colour of Burne Jones; how much of his influence is found in the work of his brother artists, Holman Hunt, Madox Brown, and Millais, and through them in all that is highest and best in present-day English art and song, we feel that to us this man brought no common gift.

He has left us a noble heritage. From the inner shrine and very treasure-house of beauty he has brought, as of old time was brought to Balaustion, glory of the golden word and passion of the picture,— or, to use his own image, there have been born to life these two children—

> "*Song*, whose hair
> Blew like a flame and blossomed like a wreath;
> And *Art*, whose eyes were worlds by God found fair."

And if, as in the perfect phrase of this sonnet, the latest birth of Life be Death, as her three first-born were Love and Art and Song, yet two that she has borne to him—Art, namely, and Song—shall not now be subject to that last, that Life and Love with it may pass away, but that very surely no death that ever may be born shall have power upon these for ever.

P. W. NICHOLSON.

www.ingramcontent.com/pod-product-compliance
Lightning Source LLC
Chambersburg PA
CBHW032138230426
43672CB00011B/2377